PRAISE FOR

"*Business Made Simp*... gaining more traction... ...over before and have clarity and purpose."

—James Thorne, Quirk Growth

"*Business Made Simple* helped me get my law practice off the ground. I learned to build and track revenue while providing quality service to my clients."

—Mariah Street, Legacy Street Law

"*Business Made Simple* helps me go into any company and make it successful."

—Samidha Singh, Student

"*Business Made Simple* is the perfect daily antidote for aspiring entrepreneurs who, in their pursuit of business success, overcomplicate, neglect, or just forget the basics."

—Donald St. George, Sherlock Aviation Consulting

"*Business Made Simple* is an essential part of my morning routine."

—Craig Dacy, Craig Dacy Financial Coaching

"Watching the *Business Made Simple* videos has been a great way to start the day. It gets me thinking about the important ideas to help me win from the first couple minutes of the day."

—Stuart Montgomery, Twin Pines Lawn Care

Donald Miller

Business Made Simple

Sixty Days to Master Leadership,
Communication, Sales, and More

HarperCollins
Leadership

An Imprint of HarperCollins

Published by HarperCollins Leadership, an imprint of HarperCollins Focus LLC.

Any internet addresses, phone numbers, or company or product information printed in this book are offered as a resource and are not intended in any way to be or to imply an endorsement by HarperCollins Leadership, nor does HarperCollins Leadership vouch for the existence, content, or services of these sites, phone numbers, companies, or products beyond the life of this book.

ISBN 978-1-4002-0382-6 (eBook)
ISBN 978-1-4002-0381-9 (HC)

Library of Congress Control Number: 2020947602

Printed in the United States of America
20 21 22 23 LSC 10 9 8 7 6 5 4 3 2 1

In memory of Brian Hampton, my publisher for fifteen years. He taught me about books and business but mostly about kindness and character. You are missed.

Feel free to read this book straight through. However, if you'd like to slowly learn the concepts in *Business Made Simple*, visit BusinessMadeSimple.com/Daily to receive a daily video that will coincide with each day's lesson. In only two months, you will get a business education many people pay tens of thousands of dollars for by attending business school. This book will transform you into somebody who has the practical skills to make and save yourself—and any organization—money. This book will teach you to lead a team, sell more product, and run a business.

Again, to *receive the daily videos that accompany the entries in this book, visit BusinessMadeSimple.com/Daily or send a blank email to:*

VIDEOS@BUSINESSMADESIMPLE.COM

To get the most from this book:

1. Watch one video per day for the next sixty days (weekends excluded).
2. Read the accompanying daily entry.
3. Practice what you've learned in your own company or the company you work for to become a value-driven professional.

* To receive daily videos in your email that align with the daily entries in this book, send a blank email to videos@businessmadesimple.com.

A Value-Driven Professional

Strategy

Communication

Messaging

Management

Execution

Leadership

Character

Negotiation

Productivity

Sales

Marketing

A solid business education should not cost tens of thousands of dollars and should focus on teaching practical skills that translate into business success. This book is designed to help you and your team become value-driven professionals. Value-driven professionals get more done in less time, create less stress and more clarity, and earn more for themselves and those they represent.

A team full of value-driven professionals is unstoppable.

"We should not trust the masses who say only the free can be educated, but rather the lovers of wisdom who say that only the educated can be free."

—EPICTETUS, *Discourses*, 2.1.21–23a

TABLE OF CONTENTS

INTRODUCTION

Two candidates are up for a promotion. The new job is a leadership position that will require a broad range of skills.

Candidate one has a college degree from a prestigious university, loves people, has demonstrated a strong work ethic, and is devoted to the company.

When asked what they will bring to the table, candidate one says they will bring passion, a good attitude, and a willingness to be a team player.

Candidate two has already read this book and watched the accompanying videos. Not only this, but they've taken a deep dive into the material and honed their skills in their previous position.

Even though they don't have a degree from a prestigious university, they know how to offer tangible value to any company.

When candidate two is asked what they will bring to the table, they say they will bring a set of core character traits that have proven to predict success. They will also bring a set of ten core competencies that will immediately make or save the company money. Listing the traits, they explain that:

1. **They know how a business really works.** They are not naive about the importance of the activity-to-output ratio and the importance of positive cash flow in each division.
2. **They are a clear and compelling leader.** They can align and inspire a team by guiding them through a process in which they create a mission statement and guiding principles.
3. **They are personally productive.** They have mastered a specific system they implement every day so they can get more done in less time.
4. **They know how to clarify a message.** They are able to guide a team through a framework in which they create a clear message promoting any product or vision so customers and stakeholders engage.
5. **They understand how to build a marketing campaign.** They can create a sales funnel that converts interested customers into buyers.
6. **They can sell.** They have mastered a framework in which they introduce products to qualified leads and consult with them until a valuable contract is signed.
7. **They are great communicators.** They can give a speech that informs and inspires a team, resulting in clear action that positively affects the bottom line.
8. **They are good negotiators.** They do not trust their gut when they negotiate. Rather, they follow a simple set of procedures that guides them to the best possible result.
9. **They are a good manager.** They know how to create a production process that is measured through key performance indicators that guarantee efficiency and profitability.

10. **They know how to run an execution system.** They have mastered a framework that ensures a high-powered team gets the right things done.

Two candidates answered the same question, but which candidate stands out?

Candidate two is going to get the promotion. And soon after, they are going to get a raise. And soon after that, they are going to get another promotion and another raise. Why? Because they have tangible skills that save their teams frustration and make themselves and the company money. In short, they are a terrific investment.

Whether you work for yourself or work for a company, giving your customers or your boss an incredible return on their investment is the key to building your personal wealth. Each of the team members in my company is a terrific investment; otherwise, they never would have been hired. And even though I own the company, I have to be a value-driven professional too. If my products and I are not a good economic investment, my career and my company are doomed. Each of us has to wake up in the morning and give people a return on the time, energy, and money they entrust to us.

This is the secret to success. If you want to succeed in work, love, friendship, and life, give the people around you a great return on whatever it is they invest in you.

In a competitive environment, every company is looking for a team member that is a good economic investment.

This book is designed to transform you into a professional of the highest economic value.

Sadly, few of the revolutionary frameworks we introduce you to in this book are skills you learned in college.

Instead of studying an ad campaign meant to sell toothpaste to suburban families in the 1970s, what if you'd learned how to manage a team, launch a product, market and sell that product, and then revise the entire process for greater efficiency?

How much more valuable would you be on the open market if you actually knew how to make a lot of money for a company?

Because so many of us have no practical, real-life, business education, we find ourselves secretly wondering if we have what it takes to do the job and are worried that any day we are going to be exposed as a fraud.

Not only that, but going back to school is too expensive and time-consuming. And, if you do go back to school, are you going to learn anything useful, or are you going to study more toothpaste ads?

The truth is, if you master the lessons introduced in this book—the ten characteristics of a value-driven professional along with the ten core competencies of a value-driven professional—you will dramatically increase your personal worth on the open market. You will also become deadly at your job.

Nobody will beat you.

Little did we know when we went off to college that the late-night parties, the roaring crowds at football games, the hours of Ping-Pong, the sleeping through lectures about global market trends, and the study groups in which we tried to predict what questions would be on the test were not going to make us more valuable on the open market.

This book will.

This is *Business Made Simple*.

What is your actual value as a working professional? Do you have the character traits and skill sets of a person who can offer extreme value to an organization? Use this book to transform your economic worth.

Business
Made
Simple

A Value-Driven Professional

* Increase your personal economic value by mastering each core competency.

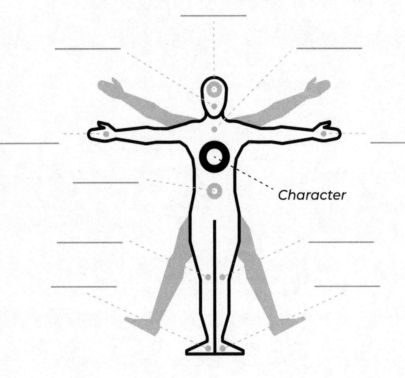

Character

CHAPTER ONE

TWO-WEEK QUICK START

The Ten Characteristics of a Value-Driven Professional

INTRODUCTION

No core competency can overcome bad character.

If we don't have good character, we are going to fail in business and in life. And we will never become value-driven professionals.

In the end, even if we can make a company money, we will likely lose them everything we made them if we lack character.

For that reason, we are going to start with a two-week dive into the character traits we need in order to add value to customers and the people we work with.

So, what are the characteristics necessary to become value-driven professionals?

Beyond integrity and a strong work ethic, how are successful people different from unsuccessful people? What is it that an individual of great economic value in the workplace believes that a person of lesser economic value does not?

In the end, a person who excels in the workforce really does see themselves differently than the average professional. And because they see themselves differently, they act differently.

As a writer, I've had the pleasure of speaking with people who offer extreme value to the world. Some of these people are well known, and some you've never heard of. But each of them excels in their job. I've been able to sit down with heads of state, professional coaches, accomplished athletes, inventors, and social justice heroes. And what I noticed about each of them is they had accepted the fact that in order to add value wherever they went, they would need to embody an uncommon set of character traits.

What follows in the next ten days are the characteristics that value-driven professionals have in common.

And the character traits I'm talking about will surprise you.

This isn't the same list you've read before, a list that starts with being diligent and working hard. When it comes to being successful, those characteristics matter, but these characteristics matter more.

For instance, every successful person I interviewed saw themselves as an economic product on the open market. They each had a strong bias toward action. None of them had a problem engaging conflict, especially when it came to matters of injustice or inequality. Each of them would rather be respected than liked. And there were many more similarities as well.

I call these characteristics *the ten characteristics of a value-driven professional*.

Who you are as a person is the foundation on which you will build the skills that will translate into tangible worth on the open market.

The great thing about the ten characteristics of a value-driven professional is they can be learned. Just reading them and watching the accompanying videos will begin to change how you see yourself and the world.

Read each entry and watch each video. The first ten days of this book will surprise, inform, and inspire you.

Again, to receive the free daily videos that accompany this book, visit BusinessMadeSimple.com/daily or send a blank email to videos@businessmadesimple.com.

DAY ONE
Character—See Yourself as an Economic Product on the Open Market

Value-driven professionals see themselves as an economic product on the open market.

How do most successful people view themselves? They view themselves as an economic product on the open market and, as mentioned in the introduction, they are obsessed with getting people a strong return on the investment made in them.

I know it sounds utilitarian to say you should view yourself as an economic product, but this simple paradigm is key to winning at work.

Of course, I am not talking about your intrinsic value as a human being. I'm talking about your value in the ecosystem that is the modern economy.

Here's the truth. People who are obsessed with being a good investment attract further investment and get to enjoy more personal economic value. When you offer greater economic value within the economic ecosystem, you are paid more, given more responsibility and promotions, and are sought after by customers looking for value. Likewise, those who resist the idea they are an economic product on the open market do not attract economic investment and so do not get to enjoy the benefits that come with giving people a great return on their investment.

Most, if not all, of the people you respect give others a terrific return on their investment. We love the athletes who perform at their best and will pay a premium to watch them compete. We love the actresses and actors who make us laugh or cry and will pay more to watch them perform. And we love the businesses who sell us products that solve whatever problem we bring to them.

Just like one of these high performers, you can become a terrific investment.

When you walk into a room, do people know instinctively they can bet on you?

How do we succeed in life and business? We prove ourselves worthy investments.

In business, your boss (or your customers) may really like you, but in large part, they see you as an economic investment. And there is nothing wrong with that. Some would even say that, when viewed this way, it's an honest relationship. After all, your friends don't pay you to be around them; your customers and teammates do.

A dream team member for any employer is a team member who actively tries to get their boss a 5X or greater return on their investment. I know that sounds crazy, but after the cost of overhead and ancillary expenditures, a 5X or greater return on a team member usually means the company narrowly makes a profit. This means if we are paid $50,000 in salary, we should be looking to make the company we work for at least $250,000 so the company itself can stay healthy and grow.

As we grow in our careers and continue to offer value, a good company will move us up and pay us more so we can continue to offer a multiple on their investment.

A smart business owner or team member will always look for ways they can make customers or the business they work for more and more money so that they can continue to be worth a percentage of a greater and greater number.

This isn't just true for team members. It's true for me as a writer and business owner. The only way I succeed is if I make other people a great deal of money. The truth is, I only get to keep a small percentage of that money.

So, how do we become ridiculously successful? By making other people absurdly successful!

The hard truth is, any team member who does not get at least a 5X return on the investment made in them is a financial risk. This means when you are chosen to take a position at a company, your boss is literally betting their own career and livelihood on your performance.

The key to moving ahead is to become the very best investment possible. If you are managing a stock portfolio and one stock is consistently outperforming the others, you'll move more of your money into that stock. The same is true when choosing which team members to promote. Leaders will always move more resources to the team members who give them the greatest return on their investment.

In his book *High Output Management*, Andrew Grove, former CEO at Intel, said, "As a general rule, you have to accept that no matter where you work, you are not an employee—you are in a business with one employee: yourself. You are in competition with millions of similar businesses. There are millions of others all over the world, picking up the pace, capable of doing the same work that you can do and perhaps more eager to do it."

Can you articulate your economic value to the organization you work for? If you're in customer service, are you able to calculate how many sales you save, how much negative chatter you help the company avoid? Do you think the company makes 5X your salary because you show up every day? If so, you're going to succeed. Everybody chases a good investment and divests themselves of bad investments. Consider that a natural law.

If you own a company, are you able to articulate how your customers get a return on their financial investment in you? Does the paint you sell last longer? Will the yard you cut save your customers time and give them a sense of pride in their home?

If you are an investment that gets a return, you will attract business, responsibilities, promotions, and greater compensation.

Successful business leaders conduct their lives so they are terrific financial investments. You should conduct your life that way too.

Wondering how to do that? The rest of this book will give you practical skills and frameworks that will dramatically increase your worth on the open market. Keep reading and keep watching the daily videos.

Here's Today's Business Made Simple Tip of the Day

Value-driven professionals see themselves as an economic product on the open market and are obsessed with giving people a great return on their investment.

DAY TWO
Character—See Yourself as a Hero, Not a Victim

A value-driven professional sees themself as a hero, not a victim.

If you asked me to predict whether somebody will be a success in life, I could do so by asking one question about them: How often do they position themselves as a victim?

What do I mean by victim? I mean: How often do they talk about themself as though they are not in control of their life or future? Do they believe fate has dealt them a bad hand? Do they believe other people are responsible for their failures? Do they believe the marketplace or the weather or the stars are conspiring against them to stop them from succeeding?

If so, they will not succeed.

The sad truth is, many people really are victims. They really do have oppressors. But the difference between being a victim and a hero is that a victim lies down while a hero rises up and succeeds against all challenges and oppressors.

Personally, I grew up poor. I spent my early childhood in government housing. Our family stood in line for government cheese. There were definitely economic factors that made it hard for our family. My father left us and never spoke to us again when my sister and I were children, and my mother had to work long hours just to keep us fed and alive. It wasn't until her final years as a professional that she even made a living wage.

But as we got older (and I confess I struggled with victim mentality and an attitude of defeatism), my mother did something incredible. In her late fifties, she went back to school and got her bachelor's and master's degrees, only to retire. Why? Because she wanted her children to know they could accomplish anything. She did not want my sister and me to believe we come from a victim legacy.

The reality is, I (as a white man) experienced great privilege in this world even though I grew up poor. Nobody ever feared the color of my skin, and doors opened for me that don't open for some. And yet it wasn't easy. All of us, though, like my mother, can transform ourselves from seeing ourselves as victims to seeing ourselves as hardworking heroes on a mission.

Never, ever let anybody keep you down by forcing you to be a victim. If you see yourself as a victim, people will either feel sorry for you or feel good about themselves while trying to rescue you, but you yourself play a bit part in the story.

But fight for your right to succeed in this world and millions will fight with you. People love to join a hero on a mission.

As you watch successful people, you'll notice most of them have a strong aversion to seeing themselves as victims. And that's a good thing.

In stories, the victim is a bit part. The victim exists in the story to make the villain look bad and the hero look good. That's it. They do not grow, change, transform, or receive any sort of recognition at the end of the story. And that's one of the many reasons you never want to play the victim.

When I say victim in this context, I really mean "victim" in quotes because many of us find ourselves playing the victim even though we aren't victims at all.

A victim is a character that has no way out. They really are in need of rescue or else they're going to be hurt in some way.

But you and I often have a way out. We tend to move into victim mode when something gets hard. Or when we are looking for some sympathy. Or when we don't want to take responsibility for our actions.

Playing the victim often means we blame our situation for our shortcomings rather than ourselves. If we don't work as hard as necessary to accomplish something, we may blame our tools or our coworkers or the short timeline. But the truth may be that we could have gotten it done if we'd just worked a little harder.

Playing the victim can be tempting. Victims are often let off the hook because they are, after all, helpless. Victims also attract resources and perhaps even a rescuer who will do the job for them.

The problem with playing the victim is it only works once. People get tired of being around "false victims" because when you're around a false victim, you end up always having to do their work for them. Eventually, a false victim is resented for stealing resources and help from actual victims.

Competent professionals can deal with any sort of challenge—even unfair challenges—and yet still find a way to win. All of us, from time to time, aren't treated fairly, but it's the heroes who overcome their oppressors to accomplish their important mission.

At the end of the movie, the victim is hauled off in an ambulance, but the hero, bloodied and torn because they battled their oppressor, is given a reward.

In life, the victim role (and we are all true victims at times in our lives) is temporary. What do we do when we are truly victims? We call out for help. Then we gather the strength necessary to transform back into a hero.

You will notice the most influential, successful people in life are quick to learn from their mistakes, eager to prove their worth without asking for charity, and fast to take responsibility for their shortcomings, hoping to prove themselves the next time they get a chance.

Victims do not lead the charge into the fight. Victims do not rescue others. Victims do not gain strength and overcome their captor. Only heroes do these things.

Only you get to decide whether you are a victim or a hero. It's not an identity I or anybody else gets to place on you. It's all about how you see yourself.

I ask that you choose not to see yourself as a victim. It will end your personal development. It's true that some people have to overcome more than others. But the more you overcome, the greater your heroic story.

If you have a challenge and are tempted to see yourself as a victim, remember this: Those who journey the farthest will arrive with the most strength. Keep fighting. Don't quit.

I confess that the fight not to see myself as a victim is an ongoing battle. In fact, a victim mentality is often my knee-jerk reaction. Whether it's in accepting constructive criticism from a friend or getting lit up by a troll on the internet, I have to remind myself I am not a victim. There are real victims in this world who need help. I am a hero trying to learn and get better because, like you, I am a hero on a mission to transform the world. I want every human being to have a business education that will transform them into a value-driven professional.

What I must do in the face of challenges, then, is to bandage my wounds and continue the fight.

So must you. Your mission is too important to suffer the victim's fate.

Play the hero.

Here's Today's Business Made Simple Tip of the Day

A value-driven professional sees themself as a hero on a mission, not a victim.

DAY THREE
Character—Know How to De-escalate Drama

A value-driven professional knows how to de-escalate drama.

Here's something you will notice about great leaders: They know how to de-escalate drama.

The better you are at keeping your cool and helping others around you keep their cool, the more respected you will be and the more you will be chosen to move up.

Unnecessary drama usually exists when a person is trying to bring attention to themself. Drama is how some people accomplish their agenda. If you don't want people to criticize you, for example, overreact to criticism by being dramatic and you'll ensure people will never criticize you again. That is, to your face. Being dramatic, sadly, will mean they criticize you all day long behind your back.

A dramatic person sucks the energy out of the room and into themselves. This is perfectly appropriate for an actor on a stage, but in real life, and especially in a business environment, it will kill your career.

Every person has a certain amount of energy to spend each day. With that energy they meet their own needs, the needs of their coworkers, and the needs of the people they care about. Dramatic people, however, steal your energy so you don't have anything left to take care of yourself or others.

For this reason, dramatic people can be off-putting, and most people try to stay away from them.

So, how do you become somebody who de-escalates rather than creates drama?

The key is to close the drama gap.

If you rate a situation on a scale of 1 to 10 regarding the drama it deserves, the key to being a balanced person is to meet the level of drama at or below its worthiness on the scale.

If somebody logged into your computer to check their personal email and forgot to log out and you respond by throwing the computer across the room, you've opened the drama gap too wide. You've overreacted.

Here's the general idea:

We respect people who react a little under, not over, the level of drama a situation deserves. We trust people who can remain calm and de-escalate drama so that crucial energy needed to deal with a truly important situation is not wasted.

Neil Armstrong, the first man to walk on the moon, developed the reputation of being unflappable in any situation. No matter what chaos was going on around him, he could land the plane and, later, help land a lunar module on the moon. When tasked with something monumental, being a dramatic person will not serve your interests.

So, how do you de-escalate drama?

A crucial question to ask during a dramatic situation is this: How would a calm and calculated person handle this situation?

You'll be amazed at how clear a right response becomes when you remove yourself emotionally from a situation and respond as though you were writing the script rather than living inside the script.

A friend once told me he was in an argument with his wife, and when he stepped outside himself to watch the scene as though it were in a movie, he realized he was being a dramatic jerk. Instead of escalating the drama, he confessed to his wife that he felt a little embarrassed about how he was acting, asked for a few minutes, and then came back and apologized.

After they made up, he was surprised to see how much more she respected him because he was able to de-escalate drama rather than fight it out until he won the argument.

The truth is, none of us has to be a slave to our emotions. Our emotions do not have to become actions.

Over time, a person who stays cool under pressure and de-escalates drama will gain respect and be chosen to lead.

Here's Today's Business Made Simple Tip of the Day

A value-driven professional de-escalates drama.

DAY FOUR
Character—Accept Feedback as a Gift

A value-driven professional knows feedback is a gift.

When we were born, people gathered around us in amazement. Everybody wanted to hold us, praise us, and celebrate our existence. Why? Because nothing is more deserving of unconditional love than a newborn baby.

As we get older, though, more is expected of us. We are taught what is safe and what is dangerous, what is appropriate and inappropriate, and later what is moral and immoral.

A mark of a competent adult is their ability to accept feedback. The mark of a child is their expectation of praise without merit.

Children get praised for simply existing while adults are expected to learn, get better, and give back.

While it can often be hard to accept feedback, especially if it is uninvited, the ability to do so is the sign of maturity and will give you a competitive advantage in the marketplace.

Those who can accept feedback from trusted mentors and friends are able to improve upon their social and professional abilities.

Many of the world's most successful people have established a routine in which they get feedback from their peers.

You, too, can establish a routine in which you get feedback about your professional performance. Could you be doing better work? Could you do better about hitting deadlines? Are there techniques you don't know about that would make you more productive or efficient? Are you annoying the people around you with unprofessional behavior?

At my company, every team member has a weekly stand-up meeting with their boss and a quarterly performance review. In these honest meetings, performance is critiqued so that their performance can improve. Then, at the end of the year, a compensation package is delivered based on that performance. Responding to feedback, then, is directly associated with their personal economic worth.

If the company you work for does not run an execution system in which you get feedback, set a quarterly meeting on your calendar with a mentor or friend who works alongside you in some capacity. Ask them for feedback. Consistently ask them where you can improve.

To establish a feedback loop in your life, consider these ideas:

1. Choose people who have your best interests at heart.
2. Schedule meetings in a repeating routine—every quarter or every month.
3. Establish a routine set of questions:

Have you seen me act unprofessionally?
Have you noticed that I've been missing something?
What am I doing that I can improve upon?
The honest observations of your trusted friends are the nutrients that will help grow your professional muscles.

After they offer feedback, ask them if they are leaving anything out. Perhaps there is something you have missed completely but need to know about in order to improve.

Thank them for the feedback and then apply what they've shared to your work. Feedback is meaningless unless it is used to help us change and take action.

Accepting and metabolizing feedback can be your secret weapon to becoming a powerful, competent professional. Very few people have the ability to hear and accept feedback. If you do, you will grow personally and professionally in ways you never imagined.

Here's Today's Business Made Simple Tip of the Day

Value-driven professionals establish a routine in which they get feedback from people they trust. They then use that feedback to grow in their career.

DAY FIVE
Character—Know the Right Way to Engage in Conflict

A value-driven professional knows the right way to engage in conflict.

Conflict-avoidant people are rarely chosen to lead.

Why? Because all human progress happens by passing through conflict. You cannot climb a mountain, build a bridge, create a community, or grow a business without engaging in and navigating conflict.

Positive ambition will always meet resistance.

A manager's primary job is to navigate conflict. Whether they're talking to an unhappy customer, letting go of an underperforming employee, reporting less-than-favorable data, or confronting a competitor, conflict and success go hand in hand.

If you avoid conflict, you will not achieve success.

So, how do we navigate conflict in such a way that we benefit ourselves and everybody around us?

Understanding these four tactics will help anybody navigate conflict in order to succeed in their careers.

1. **Expect conflict.** Conflict is a natural by-product of collaboration. When people work together, whether in a business or a society, there will be tension in sorting out how we will move forward. Conflict is not wrong; it's the by-product of progress.

2. **Control your emotions.** Conflict gets out of hand when it becomes emotional. When you feel contempt and anger for the person you are confronting, you've turned off the rational, reasonable part of your brain and are more likely to escalate drama. Try to remain calm and reasonable as you engage in conflict.

3. **Affirm the person you are confronting.** When people are confronted, they often feel threatened at the level of their identity. Make sure to make statements that affirm and respect, even as you confront.

4. **Understand you could be wrong.** Conflict increases when individuals hold their own ideas as precious. Always remember the point of conflict is progress, not proving you are right. Make the goal to move in a positive direction by collaborating with whomever you are talking with about benefiting them and their career.

A value-driven professional loves healthy conflict the way a professional athlete loves the pain of a good workout. It's through healthy conflict and tension that we make progress.

Manage conflict well and you will be given more and more responsibility.

Here's Today's Business Made Simple Tip of the Day

A value-driven professional knows how to manage conflict.

DAY SIX
Character—Long to Be Trusted and Respected More Than Liked

A value-driven professional wants to be trusted and respected more than they want to be liked.

What do team members really want from a leader?

Amateur leaders are more concerned with getting their team members to like them than they are in getting their team members to respect them. But friendship is not what team members want most from their leaders. What team members want most is clarity.

A basketball coach who wants to be liked more than they want to be respected will build a team that loses game after game.

Certainly, everybody wants to be treated with kindness and respect, but a kind, respectful leader who does not set clear expectations and coach their team toward victory is going to frustrate team members in the long run. And that frustration will cost that leader respect.

Many new managers are confused at how relationships with peers change when they are chosen to lead. People who were once friends stop confiding in them. The laughing and joking often stops when they walk into a room, and a slight distance begins to grow between them and the peers who serve on their teams.

This dynamic is natural.

This distance doesn't happen because the team has stopped liking the leader. In fact, the team often has more respect for their friend than they did before. The distance happens because suddenly disapproval from their onetime friend could cost them their job.

As you grow in your career, be careful not to take your newly earned status personally. Instead of trying to be liked (which will be tempting), earn your team members' respect.

Here are three things everybody respects in a leader:

1. **Clear expectations.** A value-driven leader focuses on the big picture, letting their team know where the company or division is going. What's the goal of the team as a whole? When you ask a team member what their boss expects of them, the team member should know; otherwise, they are not being led well.

2. **Accountability.** Is Amy in charge of turning in inventory reports every month? Is Brad expected to make fifteen sales calls per day? Let them know and keep them accountable in a daily stand-up meeting.

3. **Rewards for good performance.** Once you explain the big picture and set clear individual expectations, you'll want to affirm the team is doing a good job and challenge and support them to close performance gaps. Do not put your team in the mind-reading business. Even if they clearly meet your expectations, they won't believe it until you tell them.

When you set clear expectations, provide accountability for those expectations, and reward good performances, your team will thrive. Spend less time trying to be liked and more time giving your team clear expectations and you will earn their respect.

Here's Today's Business Made Simple Tip of the Day

A value-driven professional earns their team's respect by setting clear expectations, providing accountability, and rewarding good performances.

DAY SEVEN
Character—Have a Bias toward Action

A value-driven professional has a bias toward action.

I've never met two successful people who are the same. I've met successful people who are humble and others who are arrogant. I've met successful people who are creative and successful people who are uncreative. I've met successful people with frantic energy and others who are so at ease you wonder how they ever became successful in the first place.

Truthfully, becoming successful is more about fully being yourself than it is about any kind of formula. Different people have different superpowers, and when we fully live into our superpowers, we start seeing positive progress in our careers.

That said, there is one thing every successful person has in common: They have a bias toward action.

What I mean by a bias toward action is they do not let ideas die on the vine. They take action to make those ideas happen.

Around our office, we call this "getting the ball in the end zone." We say this because we know drawing up plays, giving pep talks, and even the hard work of driving the ball down the field does not produce points. The only thing that produces points is putting the ball in the end zone.

Successful people make real things happen in the real world. They do not let their best life get stuck in their imaginations.

In fact, it's been surprising to me how many successful people I've met who I did not find to be especially intelligent. That is, as I've talked with them, I realized they were not well read or imaginative. And as I've wondered how such simple thinkers could end up with so much influence and money, I've realized it's because of their incredibly strong bias toward action.

While others may have terrific ideas or be able to see an important issue from many angles, action-oriented people are good at getting things done.

As you attempt to build your company or your career, know that you can beat just about anybody in the marketplace as long as you wake up every day and take action.

Later, I'll show you a personal productivity framework that will help you get more done, but for now, know that daydreaming and talking about ideas do not put points on the scoreboard. It's only when we make a real thing happen in the real world that our world begins to change and get better.

> **Here's Today's Business Made Simple Tip of the Day**
>
> A value-driven professional beats the competition by having a bias toward action.

DAY EIGHT
Character—Do Not Choose to Be Confused

A value-driven professional does not choose to be confused.

Something my business coach, Doug Keim, once said to me has stuck. We were talking on the phone and I was asking about a certain employee who had been underperforming for over a year. I've come back to his words a thousand times and they've helped me make better decisions and get things done.

He said this: "Don, stop choosing to be confused."

Essentially, Doug was saying I knew full well what I needed to do; I just didn't want to do it.

I needed to let the person go. It was time.

Since then, I've learned most situations we believe are confusing are not actually confusing. In fact, what masquerades as confusion is often our desire to avoid conflict and our unwillingness to take action.

We usually know, for example, whether we need to buy something or put the money into savings. We know whether we need to apologize to somebody. We know whether or not we should be going out or going to bed. We are not actually confused. We just don't want to do the thing we need to do, and so we choose confusion to avoid responsibility.

A value-driven professional, though, is able to see the world through an objective lens, and they do not let "people pleasing," lesser desires, or conflict-avoidance affect their clarity of mind.

When's the last time you met a high-impact individual who was always confused about what they should be doing? Likely never. Successful people do not live in confusion; they live in clarity. And it's not because they see the world clearly and the rest of us don't. The truth is, we all see the world fairly clearly. We just choose to be confused.

I've found there are usually one of three reasons I am choosing to be confused:

1. **I'm people pleasing.** I worry about whether or not other people will still like me if I do what I know I need to do.
2. **I'll lose face.** I am worried about what other people (often strangers) will think of me if I do the right thing.

3. **Fear.** I fear the financial or physical consequences of doing the right thing.

It helps me in times of confusion to actually name what it is that is making me confused. Whether it's people pleasing, losing face, or fear, the confusion tends to subside the moment I give it a name.

The question we must ask ourselves in situations that seem confusing is this: If I were a different person, looking at my life from the outside, what would be the obvious right action to take?

The answer to this question will reveal what needs to happen if we were not held back by (chosen) confusion.

Here's Today's Business Made Simple Tip of the Day

A value-driven professional does not choose to be confused about the right decisions they need to make.

DAY NINE
Character—Be Relentlessly Optimistic

A value-driven professional is relentlessly optimistic.

When the overwhelming majority of life's days work out terrifically, why do we live in so much fear that things are going to go bad?

The reason is because, as human beings, we are primates. And primates are very good at assessing and avoiding threats.

Perhaps, even, too good.

Your brain is designed to keep you alive. That is its primary job. What that means is, as a primate, you are incredibly good at anticipating what could go wrong. You're good at stepping back from the edge of the roof so you don't fall off, and you're good at sensing whether or not a person is dangerous.

If you weren't good at those things, you'd likely be dead.

And we're good at a lot more than sensing physical threats. We are good at keeping ourselves from being embarrassed because being embarrassed could cost us our standing in whatever tribe we belong to. And we're good at staying away from risky endeavors in which we might fail, as failure could cost us the resources we need to survive.

It is true that people who see life through a more sensitive risk/reward lens do tend to live lives that are safer than others. They lose less because they risk less.

But they also gain less because they risk less.

If we aren't careful, our desire to avoid risk can mask itself as cynicism. When people start talking about succeeding, for example, a cynic rolls their eyes. Why? Often, it's because they are afraid to risk but don't want to admit their fear.

The truth is, while some opportunities to succeed in life don't work, some opportunities actually do, and the more relentlessly optimistic you are, the more you get to enjoy the rewards that come with trying.

By staying relentlessly optimistic, you dramatically increase the chances that at some point you will succeed. The more optimistic you are, the more you will be willing to try— and the more you try, the more often you will actually experience success.

High-impact people believe amazing things can happen. And when they try and fail, they forget their failure almost instantly because they are so excited about the next opportunity.

Show me a successful person and I will show you somebody who has failed more than most. Show me an unsuccessful person and I'll show you somebody who quit after failing a few times. It's counterintuitive, but successful people have failed more often than unsuccessful people. It's just that they had an optimistic attitude about life and got back up.

This is true in every area of life, from relationships to sports to business.

Years ago, I interviewed Pete Carroll, then in his second year as coach of the Seattle Seahawks. I asked him about a specific belief he had, which is that every time he competes, he's going to win. Whether in checkers, chess, or football, he actually believes he's going to win every contest he enters.

I couldn't help but to ask, "Coach, what happens when you lose?"

Coach leaned back in his couch and threw up his arms. "I'm shocked!" he said. "Every time. I mean, honestly, Don, I never see it coming."

"You're shocked, every time?" I asked.

"Every time. I never expect to lose."

If you think about it, Coach Carroll's philosophy is brilliant. By staying relentlessly optimistic, he sustains the energy to keep trying and to never give up. Only a year after I interviewed him, he and his Seahawks won the Super Bowl.

And the next year they went back to the Super Bowl and lost the game on the final play. I'm guessing Pete Carroll was shocked, at least for a minute, before he got excited again about the next year's opportunity.

Nothing will cost you more in life than a predetermined belief that things aren't going to work out.

Life is a game of statistics. There are no guarantees, but the more positive effort you put in, the more likely you will be to win.

Here's Today's Business Made Simple Tip of the Day

A value-driven professional knows that relentless optimism gives them a higher percentage chance of experiencing more success in work and life.

DAY TEN
Character—Have a Growth Mindset

A value-driven professional has a growth mindset.

In her book *Mindsets*, Stanford professor Carol Dweck wrote about two mindsets that, to a large degree, predict the success or failure of an individual or team. The first is a fixed mindset. Those who have a fixed mindset believe their character traits and abilities are largely unchangeable, that they are who they are and they are not capable of evolving into a better version of themselves.

People with a fixed mindset document their intelligence and abilities but do not believe they can improve on either.

Because those with a fixed mindset believe they were born with a fixed level of intelligence, they have a fear of sounding dumb in front of others. They do not believe they can learn anything new and so become defensive when they are criticized or when they fail. Why do they become defensive? Because they do not believe they can learn to do better.

The second mindset Dweck revealed was a growth mindset. Dweck found that people with a growth mindset believed their brains were adaptable and could get smarter. They were more willing to embrace challenges and did not see failure as a condemnation of their identity.

In her research with students, Dweck found those with a growth mindset sought to improve after performing poorly on tests while those with a fixed mindset gave up. Students with a growth mindset improved and earned better grades while those with a fixed mindset did not. Those with a growth mindset enrolled in more advanced classes while students with a fixed mindset were left behind.

You can easily see where all this is going. Those with a growth mindset are rewarded by being given greater levels of responsibility, experiencing greater performance, and receiving better compensation.

The good news is, transforming from a fixed to a growth mindset is possible.

To transform from a fixed mindset into a growth mindset, Dweck recommends seeing the world differently in five distinct categories:

1. **Challenges.** We must embrace challenges rather than avoid them.
2. **Obstacles.** We must persist through obstacles rather than give up.
3. **Effort.** We must see effort as a path to mastery rather than as a fruitless endeavor.
4. **Criticism.** We must learn from criticism rather than ignoring useful feedback.
5. **Success of others.** We must be inspired by the success of others rather than feeling threatened.

In short, having a growth mindset is about understanding that we will never reach the top of the mountain but we can keep climbing so the view gets better and better.

The transition from fixed to growth mindset takes us from believing "I have arrived" to "I am getting better" and from "I am great" to "I am constantly learning and improving."

Even believing you have a fixed mindset and cannot learn to have a growth mindset is a self-fulfilling prophecy. Do you have a growth mindset?

> **Here's Today's Business Made Simple Tip of the Day**
>
> A value-driven professional approaches the world with a growth mindset, believing they were designed to grow and get better in every area of life.

A Value-Driven Professional

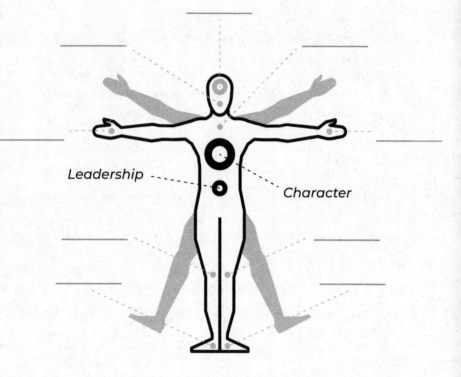

Leadership

Character

CHAPTER TWO

LEADERSHIP MADE SIMPLE

How to Create a Mission Statement and Guiding Principles

INTRODUCTION

Once you develop the character traits of a value-driven professional, you will be asked to lead. Anybody who demonstrates the character traits defined in the first two weeks of this book is going to rise above, guaranteed.

But then, how do we lead?

Well, there's a lot to leadership, and the truth is, no two leaders are alike.

But all good leaders are able to cast a vision that excites and unites a team; otherwise, their people are confused and their objectives fail.

In fact, here is leadership in a nutshell:

1. Invite a team into a story.
2. Explain why the story matters.
3. Give every team member a role to play in the story.

The number one job of a leader is to wake up every morning, point to the horizon, and let everybody on the team know where the organization is going.

The number two job of a leader is to explain, in clear and simple terms, why the story of going to and arriving at that specific destination matters.

The number three job of a leader is to analyze the skills and abilities of each team member and find them an important role to play in that story.

All human beings long for a mission. We are all born self-identifying as heroes in a story and we know, even as children, that our existence on this planet matters.

Not only this, but as communal beings, every person longs to join a team on a serious and important mission.

This is why dynamic leaders are able to attract top talent. Every dynamic leader you know or have ever heard of had a mission burning inside them that other people wanted to join.

Great leaders become great because their mission makes them great. There are no exceptions.

Teams that are not united around a compelling mission waste time, energy, and money moving in random directions that do not serve the overall objective of the organization.

Not only do people without a mission waste company resources, they waste their lives. Human beings were designed to be heroes on a mission accomplishing great things. When we accomplish important tasks, we feel important ourselves. When we don't, we sense we are not living up to our potential.

A leader who can help a team define a mission and who can remind that team daily of what the mission is and why it matters is a valuable gift to their organization.

In the next five days, I'll introduce you to the five components that make up a set of guiding principles. This set of guiding principles defines a mission that can be used to unite an entire company, or a division of that company. Many have even used the Mission Statement Made Simple framework to unite their families!

The principles I will take you through over the next five days can work for your career, your personal life, or for your family.

In my own life, I've developed a set of guiding principles (a mission) for my personal life, my marriage, our home, my company, and a set of guiding principles for a political advocacy effort I started on behalf of middle-class families.

Because of these guiding principles, I do not wake up in a fog every day. I always know what I should be working on and why.

Each set of guiding principles I'll teach you includes five components:

1. **Create a mission statement** that actually excites you.
2. **Create a set of key characteristics** that will guide your development.
3. **Create a list of critical actions** that will ensure you accomplish the mission.
4. **Create a story pitch** that attracts resources to your mission.
5. **Define a theme** that will serve as the "why" of your mission.

When complete, the guiding principles that cast a vision for yourself or an organization should all be able to fit on one simple page as in Figure 2.1.

To learn to create a set of guiding principles for you and your team, read each day's entry, watch the accompanying video you will get in your email, and create a set of guiding principles of your own.

By the end of this third week, you will learn a foundational skill that most leaders never realize. You will know how to unite a team around a mission.

Jeannie's Flower Shop

MISSION STATMENT

We bring joy to people by providing the best flowers in the Houston area because people come alive when they are given flowers by somebody they love.

KEY CHARACTERISTICS

1. Positive: We believe anybody's day can be brightened with flowers.

2. Creative: We create the most beautiful flower arrangements in Houston.

3. Dedicated: We are dedicated to our work because other people's joy depends on our work.

CRITICAL ACTIONS

1. We smile: We have an upbeat, positive attitude because flowers are all about bringing joy to others.

2. We learn: We are constantly learning about flowers and how to make better flower arrangements.

3. We clean: We clean the sales floor three times each day.

YOUR STORY PITCH

At Jeannie's Flowers we believe many people go through their days without being recognized by others. Not being recognized makes a person sad and causes them to lose hope.

When somebody gets flowers, they come alive because somebody else remembered them. A simple bouquet of flowers can remind a person how much they are cared about and brighten their spirits for days.

We provide the best flowers in the Houston area because everybody deserves a simple and effective way to recognize the people they love.

THEME

When people are recognized with flowers, they come alive.

FIGURE 2.1

To receive the videos that accompany each entry, send a blank email to VIDEOS@BUSINESSMADESIMPLE.COM and we will do the rest.

DAY ELEVEN
How to Lead—Write a Good Mission Statement

To unite and motivate a team, learn to write a *mission statement* that is short, interesting, and memorable (see Figure 2.2).

Jeannie's Flower Shop

MISSION STATMENT

We bring joy to people by providing the best flowers in the Houston area because people come alive when they are given flowers by somebody they love.

KEY CHARACTERISTICS

1. Positive: We believe anybody's day can be brightened with flowers.

2. Creative: We create the most beautiful flower arrangements in Houston.

3. Dedicated: We are dedicated to our work because other people's joy depends on our work.

CRITICAL ACTIONS

1. We smile: We have an upbeat, positive attitude because flowers are all about bringing joy to others.

2. We learn: We are constantly learning about flowers and how to make better flower arrangements.

3. We clean: We clean the sales floor three times each day.

YOUR STORY PITCH

At Jeannie's Flowers we believe many people go through their days without being recognized by others. Not being recognized makes a person sad and causes them to lose hope.

When somebody gets flowers, they come alive because somebody else remembered them. A simple bouquet of flowers can remind a person how much they are cared about and brighten their spirits for days.

We provide the best flowers in the Houston area because everybody deserves a simple and effective way to recognize the people they love.

THEME

When people are recognized with flowers, they come alive.

FIGURE 2.2

To lead yourself or a team, you have to know where you're going. You have to define a specific destination.

Most companies do this with a mission statement, but let's face it, most mission statements are *terrible*. They're full of insider language and business jargon and sound more like they were written by lawyers on behalf of shareholders than by team members who are passionate about their work.

So, how do we write a mission statement people will actually remember and execute?

If William Wallace from the movie *Braveheart* can't shout your mission statement from horseback to inspire a group of soldiers to sacrifice themselves on behalf of the mission, then it's not a very interesting mission statement.

Imagine William Wallace shouting your corporate mission statement—that is, if you even know what your mission statement is.

Hard to imagine firing up troops with your current mission statement?

Okay, then let's fix it.

A good mission statement is short, interesting, and inspirational. Otherwise, it's worthless.

In addition, your mission statement should position your effort as *a counterattack against an injustice*. It should explain what you are doing to serve people and why that effort matters.

The soldiers landing on the beaches of Normandy were on a mission. The Freedom Riders traveling across the South during the Civil Rights era were on a mission. The astronauts redefining human limitations were on a mission. As was the auto manufacturer Tesla by disrupting the combustion engine industry with electric cars and Netflix with streaming movie services. The book you are currently reading is disrupting America's business schools by teaching practical business skills in bite-sized chunks for a fraction of the cost.

People are attracted to a mission. They aren't attracted to business jargon. And, again, your business is made up of people who are looking to contribute to a mission.

Here is a formula for a good, short mission statement:

We will accomplish _____ by _____ because of _____.

Here are some examples:

A *plumbing company:* We will service ten thousand customers within the next five years because everybody deserves plumbing that works and service that makes them feel valued.

A *software company:* Our software will run on half the computers in America by 2029 because nobody should have to suffer a software interface that confuses them.

A *family restaurant:* We will be known as the best pizza in the state within five years because people in our community deserve to brag about pizza made with local ingredients.

Simple mission statements like these inspire action. And because we've included a deadline, it also creates a sense of urgency.

Once the deadline is reached, by the way, you just rewrite the mission statement. There's no reason a mission statement can't be re-created every few years.

You certainly don't have to use this formula to write a mission statement, but be honest, these are a lot more clear and motivating than most of the mission statements organizations are using today.

In fact, most mission statements are completely forgettable. Do you even know yours? Does anybody on your team even remember your mission statement?

I once sat in a conference room with a group of executives who pushed back hard when I said most mission statements are terrible. They'd recently participated in a forty-eight-hour retreat in which they had painstakingly chosen every word of their new mission statement.

I pointed at the CFO and asked if he'd been on the retreat. He said he had. I asked him to recite the mission statement, but he couldn't. He'd forgotten it.

The reality is, if we or our teams cannot recite our mission statement, we are not on a mission. We've forgotten a mission.

Competent team members know how to motivate themselves and unite a team around a mission statement.

Just remember, keep it short, keep it interesting, and make it inspirational.

Your mission statement is the first part of a five-part set of guiding principles. In the next four days, I'll take you through the remaining components that will guide, align, and inspire your team.

> ### Here's Today's Business Made Simple Tip of the Day
>
> To unite a team, create a set of guiding principles that includes a mission statement that is short, interesting, and memorable.

DAY TWELVE
How to Lead—Define Key Characteristics

Define the key characteristics you'll need to develop in order to accomplish your mission and you'll transform yourself and your team.

The second component in your set of guiding principles is your *key characteristics* (see Figure 2.3).

Jeannie's Flower Shop

MISSION STATMENT

We bring joy to people by providing the best flowers in the Houston area because people come alive when they are given flowers by somebody they love.

KEY CHARACTERISTICS

1. Positive: We believe anybody's day can be brightened with flowers.

2. Creative: We create the most beautiful flower arrangements in Houston.

3. Dedicated: We are dedicated to our work because other people's joy depends on our work.

CRITICAL ACTIONS

1. We smile: We have an upbeat, positive attitude because flowers are all about bringing joy to others.

2. We learn: We are constantly learning about flowers and how to make better flower arrangements.

3. We clean: We clean the sales floor three times each day.

YOUR STORY PITCH

At Jeannie's Flowers we believe many people go through their days without being recognized by others. Not being recognized makes a person sad and causes them to lose hope.

When somebody gets flowers, they come alive because somebody else remembered them. A simple bouquet of flowers can remind a person how much they are cared about and brighten their spirits for days.

We provide the best flowers in the Houston area because everybody deserves a simple and effective way to recognize the people they love.

THEME

When people are recognized with flowers, they come alive.

FIGURE 2.3

As you set out on your mission, you're inviting people into a story in which they overcome challenges in order to accomplish something great. And in stories, characters change. They become stronger, better equipped, more confident, and more competent to do the job at hand.

It is through living a meaningful story that we transform into better versions of ourselves.

When you list the key characteristics you and your people will need to embody in order to accomplish your mission, you're basically telling everybody on the team who they need to become.

What characteristics do you and your team need to develop in order to accomplish your mission? Do you need to become faster, more attentive to customers, better coders?

When you define the key characteristics you and your team need to develop, make sure they are both aspirational and instructive.

When I say aspirational, I mean they don't have to be characteristics you currently embody. They can be characteristics that demand improvement and change. And when I say instructive, what I mean is they should be immediately actionable when somebody hears them. *A positive attitude* is instructive, as is *disciplined about making sales calls* or *quick to greet customers at the door.* If your key characteristics are too vague, team members will not know how to act on them and so they won't inspire change.

If your mission is to find homes for the number of neglected dogs in your area, a key characteristic of the people on your team should be that they love to be around dogs. If your mission is to create software that makes managing money easy, a key characteristic should be that your people are students of great software interfaces.

A recent quick-serve restaurant we worked with is known for their positive environment. Every day they open their door to a line of people who have been waiting for hours to eat their fried chicken. And while they're a huge hit, their challenge is to keep up that positive attitude under such intense pressure.

For this reason, they defined one of their key characteristics as being *fun under pressure.*

This key characteristic was brilliant because it serves our two purposes:

1. **It is aspirational.** It helps the team know the kind of people they need to become in order to achieve the mission.
2. **It is instructive.** It tells the team the kind of people they need to be when the pressure gets high.

Whenever the kitchen is backed up, they've run out of a specific ingredient, and a bus full of tourists just pulled up, how should our friends at the restaurant respond? They should respond by having fun under pressure.

Can you imagine how much negativity and drama is up-ended by defining a key characteristic such as *fun under pressure*?

When you define the key characteristics your team needs to develop, you're defining the kind of people who are allowed to work for you. If somebody at the restaurant is not fun under pressure, for instance, they are not a fit.

Defining key characteristics helps you know which people to hire and which people to dismiss. If you fail to define the key characteristics required to accomplish your mission, you will likely have the wrong people on your team.

What sort of characteristics is it important for you and your team members to have in order to accomplish your mission? Who do you and your people need to become?

Here's Today's Business Made Simple Tip of the Day

As part of your set of guiding principles, define the key characteristics you and your team need to develop in order to accomplish your mission.

DAY THIRTEEN
How to Lead—Determine Critical Actions

Define three repeatable *critical actions* every person in your organization can take that will contribute to your mission (see Figure 2.4).

Jeannie's Flower Shop

MISSION STATMENT

We bring joy to people by providing the best flowers in the Houston area because people come alive when they are given flowers by somebody they love.

KEY CHARACTERISTICS

1. Positive: We believe anybody's day can be brightened with flowers.

2. Creative: We create the most beautiful flower arrangements in Houston.

3. Dedicated: We are dedicated to our work because other people's joy depends on our work.

CRITICAL ACTIONS

1. **We smile:** We have an upbeat, positive attitude because flowers are all about bringing joy to others.

2. **We learn:** We are constantly learning about flowers and how to make better flower arrangements.

3. **We clean:** We clean the sales floor three times each day.

YOUR STORY PITCH

At Jeannie's Flowers we believe many people go through their days without being recognized by others. Not being recognized makes a person sad and causes them to lose hope.

When somebody gets flowers, they come alive because somebody else remembered them. A simple bouquet of flowers can remind a person how much they are cared about and brighten their spirits for days.

We provide the best flowers in the Houston area because everybody deserves a simple and affective way to recognize the people they love.

THEME

When people are recognized with flowers, they come alive.

FIGURE 2.4

Most sets of guiding principles are forgotten because they don't inspire action. But unless characters in stories actually *do* something, the mission will never be accomplished.

Including critical actions in your set of guiding principles will get you and your team moving.

After we define our mission statement and key characteristics, we must move the story forward by defining the critical actions our people need to take every day to make the mission happen.

Of course, every team member has a different list of actions to take, but by defining three critical actions every one of you can take, you create a sense of alignment you would not otherwise feel.

Not only this, but by defining three critical actions every person on your team can take every day, you collect and focus energy toward the accomplishment of your mission.

For instance, if one of our critical actions is to "have a stand-up meeting every morning fifteen minutes before we open," we will all get to work early and know what our priorities are when the doors open.

What actions can every single member of your team (or division) take every day that will translate into greater productivity, more revenue, higher customer satisfaction, or a better activity-to-output ratio?

The critical actions you define for yourself and your organization should establish a way of life that affects the bottom line.

In my personal guiding principles, my repeatable critical actions are that I get up early, I write, and I say "after you."

They may sound funny, but by getting up early, I virtually ensure I get to bed early the night before, increase the chances I will exercise, get more writing done (because I write in the morning), and get some quiet time in the morning. If I write every day, I ensure my career and company continue to grow. And if I say "after you" in my comings and goings with people, I'll be sure to put others first and won't become a jerk.

Those three critical actions establish a way of life that if repeated day in and day out ensures success.

By the way, I recommend no more than three critical actions. Any more than three and people tend to forget to take action on any of them.

What repeatable, critical actions would set you and your people up for success?

What are the small critical actions you and your team can take every day to propel the mission forward? Are they simple and easy to execute? Are they repeatable? Will they actually affect the mission?

> **Here's Today's Business Made Simple Tip of the Day**
>
> Define three critical actions you and your team can take every day that will ensure success and help you accomplish your mission.

DAY FOURTEEN
How to Lead—Tell a Great Story

Know how to attract people to your mission by telling your story.

Telling the story of your company or project is important because in telling your story you attract resources. When you tell your story, people decide whether or not to buy from you, invest in you, or even spread word about what you're doing.

Most people and most companies, though, do not know how to tell their story. Often, they make the mistake of telling their *history*, complete with bullet points and boring asides.

But your history is not your story. Your story is different. Your story is a way of explaining what you do that engages people and makes them want to join. Your history, on the other hand, is just a bunch of things that have happened in your past.

The fourth aspect in your set of guiding principles is called The Story Pitch (see Figure 2.5). The reason you want a story pitch is it allows you and everybody on your team to tell the story of your business in such a way that you will be remembered and people will want to engage.

Jeannie's Flower Shop

MISSION STATMENT	KEY CHARACTERISTICS	CRITICAL ACTIONS
We bring joy to people by providing the best flowers in the Houston area because people come alive when they are given flowers by somebody they love.	1. Positive: We believe anybody's day can be brightened with flowers. 2. Creative: We create the most beautiful flower arrangements in Houston. 3. Dedicated: We are dedicated to our work because other people's joy depends on our work.	1. We smile: We have an upbeat, positive attitude because flowers are all about bringing joy to others. 2. We learn: We are constantly learning about flowers and how to make better flower arrangements. 3. We clean: We clean the sales floor three times each day.

YOUR STORY PITCH

At Jeannie's Flowers we believe many people go through their days without being recognized by others. Not being recognized makes a person sad and causes them to lose hope.

When somebody gets flowers, they come alive because somebody else remembered them. A simple bouquet of flowers can remind a person how much they are cared about and brighten their spirits for days.

We provide the best flowers in the Houston area because everybody deserves a simple and effective way to recognize the people they love.

THEME

When people are recognized with flowers, they come alive.

FIGURE 2.5

Any leader who can invite customers and stakeholders into the story of the company they represent is placed out front and given more responsibility.

And any sales professional who can invite customers into a story brings in more revenue for the company.

And any customer service representative who can invite customers into the story the business is telling creates passionate fans of the brand.

Most companies, however, tell a boring story. The truth is, very few people care how the company got started and that you've maintained a high great-places-to-work metric. A good story filters out all the noise and only highlights what is actually interesting to an audience. And a competent professional knows how to tell a story. Especially the story of their mission.

In the most simple form of story structure, a story features a character who has been destabilized by an event and then overcomes a series of challenges to restabilize their life.

This is the story line for *Star Wars*, *Romeo and Juliet*, *Tommy Boy*, all the Avengers movies, and any rom-com you can name. Why do storytellers use this formula? Because it's the most powerful tool in the world to captivate an audience's attention.

Sadly, your history may or may not break down into that formula, which is why telling your history, rather than your story, will likely bore an audience and send your customers straight to the competition.

So, if we want to tell our story, the story of our business (or the division of the business we work in), let's borrow from the same formula that has worked for thousands of years.

When you tell your story, do this:

1. Start with the problem you or your company helps people overcome.

2. Agitate that problem to make it even worse.
3. Position yourself, your company, or your product as the resolution to the problem.
4. Describe the happy ending people will experience if they use your product to resolve their problem.

This simple formula has been proven over and over to engage an audience. When you filter the "facts" of your company through this story formula, all that's left is the good stuff.

For instance, let's say you run a pet boarding business. You might tell your story this way:

Most people hate leaving their pet at a kennel when they travel. They feel guilty as they picture their lovable pup's sad eyes watching and waiting behind the bars of a cage until they return.

At Pet-Paws Paradise, we play with your pet for at least eight hours each day so they are constantly preoccupied and happy while you travel. They go to bed each night exhausted, dreaming of all the fun they had that day.

When you leave your pet with us, you know your pet is safe and happy so you can feel great like the terrific pet owner you are!

Do you see the formula? We started with a problem, made the problem worse, positioned the product as the resolution to the problem, and then described a happier life because the problem had been solved.

That's a story that will attract customers, investors, and more. That story can be spoken by salespeople, used as narration over a video, printed in small print on the back of business cards, used on websites and in promotional emails, and even used to open and close a speech given by the CEO.

If you want to be a company of great storytellers, learn to tell a story that is inviting to customers.

Recently, one of the world's largest social media companies hired us to help them convert their massive sales staff into great storytellers. The formula we taught them wasn't all that different from the formula you just learned.

Telling stories isn't hard. It just takes a little knowledge and then the discipline to stay on message.

Do you know how to tell the story of your product or business?

What problem does your company solve? How is that problem making people feel? How is your product positioned to solve that problem? And after that problem is solved, what do people's lives look like?

Answer those questions, in that order, and you'll tell the story of yourself, your business, the division of your business, or your product in such a way that people will want to engage.

Stop telling your history and start telling your story.

A competent, value-driven professional knows how to tell an interesting story. Write down the story of your business as a story pitch and include it in your set of guiding principles. Also, make sure each team member knows how to tell the story of your organization so word starts to spread and revenue goes up!

Here's Today's Business Made Simple Tip of the Day

Use our story formula to tell your story, and you will engage more people in your mission.

DAY FIFTEEN
How to Lead—Define Your Theme and Your "Why"

Define the theme of your mission so you and your people will know why your work is important.

The final element of your guiding principles is your theme. As you can see in Figure 2.6, the theme is the foundation of your entire mission. The theme is the *why* of you or your organization.

Nobody wants to contribute to a mission that isn't important. So how do we convince people our mission matters? We do this by defining a theme.

For centuries, playwrights, novelists, and, more recently, screenwriters have defined a theme for their stories. A storyteller will define their theme, mainly, to keep them on track as they write their story.

If a bit of dialogue or a certain scene does not support the theme, they cut it out of the story.

The theme of *Schindler's List*, for example, is that every human being has infinite value and should be saved. As the screenwriters wrote the screenplay, they had to filter every scene through that central idea.

When a writer defines a theme, their story gets more meaningful and more clear.

If we want our mission to be meaningful and clear, it must have a theme.

For a business (which, not unlike storytellers, is inviting an audience into a story), a theme can be anything from *nobody should have to pay too much for a new roof* to *every family deserves a vacation they will never forget*.

When you define your theme, you and everybody else will know why your mission matters.

Jeannie's Flower Shop

MISSION STATMENT

We bring joy to people by providing the best flowers in the Houston area because people come alive when they are given flowers by somebody they love.

KEY CHARACTERISTICS

1. Positive: We believe anybody's day can be brightened with flowers.

2. Creative: We create the most beautiful flower arrangements in Houston.

3. Dedicated: We are dedicated to our work because other people's joy depends on our work.

CRITICAL ACTIONS

1. We smile: We have an upbeat, positive attitude because flowers are all about bringing joy to others.

2. We learn: We are constantly learning about flowers and how to make better flower arrangements.

3. We clean: We clean the sales floor three times each day.

YOUR STORY PITCH

At Jeannie's Flowers we believe many people go through their days without being recognized by others. Not being recognized makes a person sad and causes them to lose hope.

When somebody gets flowers, they come alive because somebody else remembered them. A simple bouquet of flowers can remind a person how much they are cared about and brighten their spirits for days.

We provide the best flowers in the Houston area because everybody deserves a simple and effective way to recognize the people they love.

THEME

When people are recognized with flowers, they come alive.

FIGURE 2.6

Business Made Simple's mission is to disrupt the current education model with an easily accessible business curriculum allowing anybody to succeed at work. So, what's our theme? It's that *everybody deserves a life-changing business education.*

A tip to help you define your theme is to add the word "because" to the end of your mission statement, and then finish the sentence. We have created an accessible business curriculum because *everybody deserves a life-changing business education.*

If you ask yourself why you should get up early and go to work, the theme of your mission should serve as the answer. Personally, I get up and go to work because *everybody deserves a life-changing business education.*

Again, knowing your theme becomes important because it is the critical sound bite that answers the question *why.* Why should investors invest? Why should a recruit come and work for you? Why should customers tell their friends about your products? Define your theme, and each of those questions will have a solid answer.

Once you define your theme, paint it on the side of the break room in your building, include it on your website, turn it into a banner at your recruiting booth, and make sure everybody in the organization has it memorized. Your theme is your purpose, and people need a purpose in order to passionately engage in their work.

Why does *your* mission matter? Why is your mission worthy of sacrifice or investment? Why should others contribute to your mission? Why should your customers choose you over another brand?

Define your theme and you'll know why.

> ### Here's Today's Business Made Simple Tip of the Day
>
> Define the theme of your business so that you, your team, and your customers will know why your work matters.

A Value-Driven Professional

* *Increase your personal economic value by mastering each core competency.*

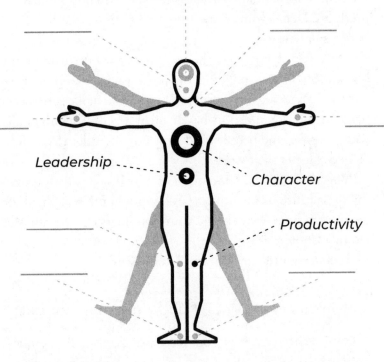

CHAPTER THREE

PRODUCTIVITY MADE SIMPLE

INTRODUCTION

Now that we've learned the character of a value-driven professional, how a business really works, and how to unite and align a team, it's time to learn how to manage ourselves and our time so we get the most done in the least amount of time and don't burden ourselves with undue stress and anxiety.

Many professionals work hard but get little done. Their frantic activity only serves to move them around in circles. There is one reason for this and it's that their life lacks focus.

In all my years studying story, I came to believe that a human being's life has the most meaning when they live it as though they are a hero on a mission. When we are a hero on a mission, we have little room for frantic activity. We know what we want, what opposes us, and what we must accomplish to solve some of the world's problems.

A hero on a mission lives with purpose and intention. They do not waste their time because their time is important. A hero on a mission knows how to manage their time so they do not feel anxious but are focused, motivated, and inspired to do the work that matters.

One of the keys to accomplishing more of the right objectives is to know what those objectives are and then know what your highest return opportunities are and to prioritize those above all others.

Value-driven professionals are heroes on a mission. They know what they should be working on and do not get distracted.

For this reason, we created the Business Made Simple Daily Planner. Because you got this book, you can get one for free at HeroOnaMission.com. The planner will guide you through a morning ritual that will help you organize your mind and plan your day. You don't have to wake up in a fog ever again.

For the next five days, I'll take you through each section of the day planner.

The truth is, our brains do not like to be confused about how we are supposed to spend our time. Not being confused, though, takes discipline and focus.

If we don't establish priorities and healthy routines, television, news, food, alcohol, and bad company are more than willing to occupy our time. Plenty of people make plenty of money by keeping us distracted. But their distractions profit you nothing.

To be a productive person, we need to give ourselves a mission and then we need to prioritize our time and objectives to accomplish our mission.

We need a framework for managing our priorities and our time.

If you want to be a value-driven professional, learn a daily routine that increases your output without increasing your anxiety. It's a winning combination. And it's not so hard to learn.

Again, this week, I will be guiding you through a daily planner page you can get for free at HeroOnaMission.com. Print out as many pages of the planner as you like, three-hole-punch them, and you've got a planner you can refill for free for life. You can continue to use the planner for decades to come. Read the daily entries this week and watch each video to learn how to fill in the planner as a morning ritual.

DAY SIXTEEN
How to Be Productive—Make Wise Daily Decisions

A productive professional starts the day with reflection.

Every morning I ask myself one simple question. This question ensures I will not let the day get away from me and that I will make progress on my goals.

The question is this: If this were the second time I were living this day, what would I do differently? (See Figure 3.1.)

At first it sounds like a crazy question. We don't get to live each day over again. We get one chance at each day.

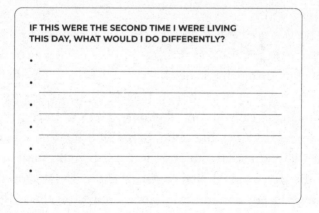

IF THIS WERE THE SECOND TIME I WERE LIVING THIS DAY, WHAT WOULD I DO DIFFERENTLY?

FIGURE 3.1

* From the free *Business Made Simple* daily planner at HeroOnAMission.com

But the question comes from Dr. Viktor Frankl and it's quite profound. Dr. Frankl was a Viennese psychologist who helped his patients by guiding them toward a deeper sense of personal meaning in their lives.

In helping his patients live with more wisdom and discretion, he asked them to live as if they were already living that day for the second time, as if they had acted wrongly the first time and were about to relive the day having learned from that day the first time around.

In other words, Frankl said, "Pretend this is the second time you lived this day and don't make the same mistakes."

This momentary pause helps us think about our lives with careful consideration. If this were the second time you lived this day and you could learn from the first, what would you do differently? Would you be more considerate to your spouse? Would you spend some time in the hammock in the backyard reading a book? Would you exercise?

Another way to word Frankl's question is this: At the end of the day, what will you have regretted doing or not doing?

Then, we need to live in such a way that we won't have regret.

Few people reflect on their actions before they take them. Most of us are moving so quickly through life and have become so accustomed to interruptions that demand our response we are no longer really in control of our own experiences.

I've met very few high-impact people who do not journal or in some way take time to reflect. It's by reflecting that we edit our actions and design our lives. Those who do not reflect neither edit nor design—they simply respond. The sad truth about this reality is their lives are still being designed—they're just being designed by outside forces that do not have their best interests at heart. Most people's life stories are dictated by friends, family, corporate commercials, or politicians with an agenda. It's time to take control of your own story.

Is there a single question you answer at the beginning of each day that causes you to pause and reflect? Are you designing your life, or is somebody else designing it for you?

> ## Here's Today's Business Made Simple Tip of the Day
>
> Create a routine of reflection by asking yourself the morning question: *If I were living this day for the second time around, what would I do differently?*

DAY SEVENTEEN
How to Be Productive—Prioritize Your Primary Tasks

A value-driven professional knows how to prioritize their highest return opportunity.

What's the most important thing you can do today?

If you can answer that question, morning after morning, you are in an elite group of professionals.

Most professionals never even ask the question because they assume the ringing phone, frustrated customer, urgent message, or neglected email is the answer. But is it?

The reality is, not every unit of work gets the same return. If you spend a bunch of calories running around in a circle, you won't get as much value from that energy as you would planning that important speech. The amount of calories you burn may be the same, but the return on your investment differs dramatically.

A value-driven professional knows where to invest hard-earned calories and what work to avoid or delegate. And because they know these things, they do not feel anxiety about their work. They are good and calm managers of their time and energy.

A value-driven professional knows how to spend their time.

The secret to focusing on your highest return opportunities involves creating two task lists each day (see Figure 3.2 and Figure 3.3). One of your task lists will be limited to three items. These three items are the most important tasks for the success of your important objectives. No matter what happens, these should be the three things you get done first.

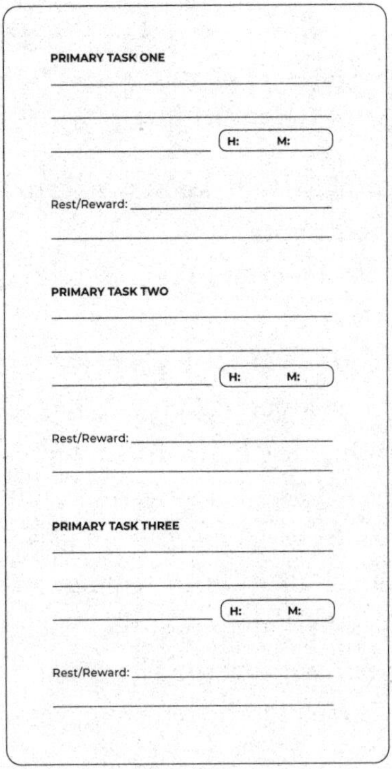

PRIMARY TASK ONE

_____

_____

_____ [H: M:]

Rest/Reward: _____

_____

PRIMARY TASK TWO

_____

_____

_____ [H: M:]

Rest/Reward: _____

_____

PRIMARY TASK THREE

_____

_____

_____ [H: M:]

Rest/Reward: _____

_____

FIGURE 3.2

SECONDARY TASKS

☐ _____ ☐ _____
☐ _____ ☐ _____
☐ _____ ☐ _____
☐ _____ ☐ _____
☐ _____ ☐ _____
☐ _____ ☐ _____

FIGURE 3.3

The other task list will be the odds and ends that need to be accomplished before the day is done. These are tasks such as returning emails, picking up your dry cleaning, and such.

The reason you want to make two lists is because your mind will not know the difference between what is very important and the random tasks that need to be done at some point in the near future. A value-driven professional knows the difference between primary and secondary tasks.

Picking up your dry cleaning should not be considered as important as working on the important presentation you will be delivering at the upcoming staff event.

My priority tasks, for example, are normally about creating some form of content. I work on a book or a business course or presentation every day, and only after I finish that writing session will I begin to return calls and engage in meetings. Each morning I write down the three pieces of content I need to work on, then I write down the secondary items jostling for my attention, and I get started on the important three items first.

Separating my three priorities has helped me grow a successful company much faster than I would have had I lumped all my tasks together.

The reason we only want to list three prioritized tasks is because listing more than three will feel too burdensome and will likely make you want to quit before you begin. Most of my prioritized tasks are small parts of much larger projects. If I'm writing a book, for example, it will take me more than a year to finish, so I need to prioritize little pieces of that book every day.

When working on enormous projects that we cannot finish in a short period of time, we are especially susceptible to short-term wins. I'd much rather return ten emails than write ten paragraphs in a book because each email makes me feel like I accomplished something while those ten paragraphs feel like a drop in a bucket.

But don't be fooled. It's by taking small steps toward big goals that we accomplish our important objectives.

Beware. Many tasks will present themselves as important, but they are not. You may get word about something that feels urgent, but the truth is that it's somebody else's job to handle it. Somebody may be coercing you into a meeting, but the truth is that meeting doesn't serve your highest priorities.

I like to call these temptations "urgent distractions" because they feel urgent but are truly just distractions.

Every day, we must always know what our three highest return opportunities are, or else low-return opportunities will feel more important.

So, how do you know what your highest return opportunities are? To know what our highest return opportunities are, we need to reverse engineer our overall objectives. Any work that moves us closer to our objectives is a high-return opportunity, and any work that does not is not. A value-driven professional knows the difference.

As it relates to being a good economic investment, what is the most important thing you need to do? What can you do that gets the company the greatest economic return? Prioritize those tasks, day after day, and you will move closer to your goals without falling into the trap of "urgent distractions."

> ### Here's Today's Business Made Simple Tip of the Day
>
> Every day make two task lists. List three items that are your highest return opportunities and then create a separate list of tasks that are not as important as your three highest priorities.

DAY EIGHTEEN
How to Be Productive—Maximize Your "Power Hours"

A value-driven professional knows to prioritize their important work for the morning.

Everybody's brain works a little bit differently, but for most people, especially people over twenty-five, their best work gets done in the morning.

Your brain is like a smartphone battery. Specifically, your brain burns between six hundred and eight hundred calories each day processing the information necessary for your survival. While you sleep, your brain recharges and is ready to face the following day.

The mental energy you have in the morning is stronger and more alert than the energy you'll have after lunch.

If you take a call or start responding to random emails before starting on your most pressing project, you're giving valuable mental energy to low-return opportunities and likely wasting the most valuable hours of your day. Later, when you finally "have time" to get to the important stuff, your brain is already tired and you're unable to do your best work (see Figure 3.4).

Not only this, but if you block time for your important projects in the morning, you get to spend the rest of the day knowing you've already completed the important tasks.

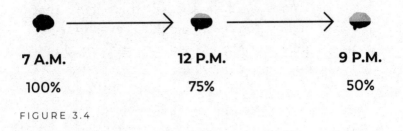

7 A.M.   **12 P.M.**   **9 P.M.**

100%   75%   50%

FIGURE 3.4

Most value-driven professionals get their important work done in the morning.

If meetings deplete your energy, schedule them in the afternoon. If processing invoices is the most important task you have, process them in the first two hours of the day before you check your email. If working on business strategy is the primary task, spend the first hour of the day refining your strategy and then start taking calls.

While the idea of prioritizing your important tasks for the morning may sound trivial, many value-driven professionals have discovered this single strategy to be a secret superpower. While their coworkers walk into the office and immediately fall into the trap of distraction, the value-driven professional has already been up for a couple of hours tackling their most important tasks. That sort of discipline and competency is going to result in trust being earned from both customers and coworkers. And that means more respect, more money, and a more enjoyable career.

> **Here's Today's Business Made Simple Tip of the Day**
>
> Prioritize your highest-return opportunities for the morning, when your mind is fresh.

DAY NINETEEN
How to Be Productive—Say "No" to Distractions

A value-driven professional knows how to say no to distractions so they can say yes to priorities.

The greatest lesson I've learned about growing a company actually came from my career as an author. The advice was this: A great communicator knows what to leave out.

It's counterintuitive, isn't it? You'd think a great communicator would know what to say, and of course they do, but the harder part is that once they say the right thing, they have to stop themselves from saying anything else.

If you're writing a book about a hero disarming a bomb, you can't include a few interesting scenes about how the hero also wants to run a marathon and marry their sweetheart and perhaps adopt a cat. If you included all that stuff in the story, you'd lose the plot. A good story can't be about too many things. Otherwise, the audience would be confused and lose interest.

That, by the way, is how most people feel about their lives. They feel like they've lost the plot. Why? Because their lives lack focus. They've said yes to so many things that they've become confused about what their story is about. And many of them are losing interest in their lives—and, for that matter, in life itself. Heroes on a mission, however, are focused.

In a good story, the writer focuses the plot on a single defined objective. The team must win the championship. The woman must get the promotion. The lawyer must win the court battle. And as tempting as other ideas may be, a good writer will say "no."

Of course, in real life, it's not that easy. As mothers, fathers, daughters, sons, friends, managers, coaches, and leaders, we really do juggle a great many subplots. There are friends who want to get together and opportunities that, while not in line with our goals, are truly exciting.

But if we say yes to too many things, we are saying no to the deep and focused attention it takes to do a few things well.

Early in my career, I made my money through public speaking. I would be paid a decent amount every time I flew somewhere and gave a speech. Soon I realized that the more I spoke, the less I was able to write. And without releasing a book every couple years, fewer people would think of me when they were choosing a speaker.

I had to make a strategic decision to turn down good money speaking in order to stay home and write more books. It was a scary decision, but that's what I did. Within two years, though, I had another bestseller and was able to charge four times my initial speaking fee whenever I left town. The result was more time at home to write, less time onstage, but a larger income.

It turns out I'm not alone. Stephen King hardly takes any speaking events at all. This is the primary reason he's been able to write so many books. King has sold tens of millions of books and could fill his schedule with lucrative meetings and speaking events, but he doesn't. Each morning he shows up at his desk, turns on his computer, and writes his daily quota of words. And because of this discipline, and the thousands of times he's said "no" to terrific opportunities, millions of readers know and love his work.

Few people realize that one of the keys to Stephen King's success is his disciplined ability to reject distracting opportunities in exchange for accomplishing his priorities.

If we don't know what our priorities are, we will say yes to everything and delude our stories so much that our lives and work no longer make sense.

What are you saying no to in order to say yes to a focused and meaningful life?

> ### Here's Today's Business Made Simple Tip of the Day
>
> Say no to distractions so you have the freedom to say yes to your priorities.

DAY TWENTY
How to Be Productive—Block Your Time and Get More Done

A value-driven professional knows how to block their time.

Bill Gates is never late to a meeting. When asked why, he said, "Because time is the one finite resource I can't buy more of."

The old proverb "time is money" isn't exactly correct. Time is worth much more than money. Time is, literally, life. And what we do with our time determines the quality of our life.

Sadly, most people do not give much thought to managing their time. That doesn't mean their time isn't managed. It's certainly managed. It's managed by television, school schedules, coercive relationships, commercialism, and work.

We would never let other people manage the money in our wallet, so why would we let other people manage our time—which, as pointed out, is worth so much more than money?

A value-driven professional knows time is their most precious commodity, and so they manage their time to bring the greatest return on their time investment. And because life is not all about work, a value-driven professional knows how to block their work time to get the most done so they can spend more of their precious time with friends, family, and enjoying hobbies.

So, how do we manage our time?

I view time like the multiple lanes of a freeway. Some lanes really do move faster than others. For the most part, if we can get all the way over on the left side of the freeway, we will move more quickly. The constant entrances and exits on the right side of the freeway mean traffic has to move more slowly.

Blocking periods of time in which you cannot be distracted is the equivalent of getting into the fast lane and pressing the gas pedal.

After your morning ritual of reflection and committing to your highest priorities, continue to block your time for the rest of the day (see Figure 3.5). In one-, two-, and three-hour chunks, you can accomplish a great deal. Multitasking, however, or simply letting the day's distractions dictate your direction, results in less productivity.

Your entire career is based on increasing output as it re-lates to your activity. A value-driven professional can get twice as much done in the same period of time as a professional who does not use time strategically.

High-performance professionals block their time weeks in advance. For me, all day Monday, Tuesday until noon, and Wednesday until noon are reserved for writing. Early after-noons on Tuesday and Wednesday are reserved for meetings, and Thursdays and half of Fridays are reserved for podcast

APPOINTMENTS

7 : 30	Work on new writing project
__ : __	_____
__ : __	_____
__ : __	_____
__ : __	_____
__ : __	_____

FIGURE 3.5

and video recordings. I also block out Friday afternoon for personal time and evenings and weekends for friends and family.

Blocking my time in advance allows me to say no to distractions because, well, I'm already booked. There is somewhere I have to be and something I need to do well in advance of that day getting started.

The idea is to create a rhythm of productivity. Once you know what your highest return opportunities are, you can block your week into chunks, allowing you to get those things done.

What important tasks do you need to do each week? Consider assigning those tasks to a specific block of time you decide in advance. Also, block personal time so you don't accidentally book a business meeting during the time block you've allotted for friends and family. Blocking your time ensures that you get more of it, while trusting your time to fate is akin to giving it away.

Here's Today's Business Made Simple Tip of the Day

Value-driven professionals know how to block their time and create a rhythm of productivity.

A Value-Driven Professional

* *Increase your personal economic value by mastering each core competency.*

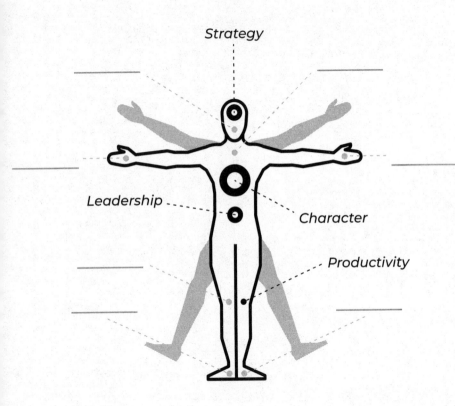

Strategy

Leadership

Character

Productivity

CHAPTER FOUR

BUSINESS MADE SIMPLE

How a Business Really Works and How to Keep It from Crashing

INTRODUCTION

Now that we've learned the character traits of a value-driven professional along with the important elements of casting a vision and becoming a more personally productive professional, I'm going to introduce you to a perspective on business that is normally understood by only the highest-level executives.

Regardless of whether you lead a team or not, your personal value as a professional will rise if you demonstrate a general understanding of how a business works. Surprisingly, many professionals who have spent years in business think they know how a business works but they don't. Instead of understanding business as a for-profit entity that solves problems for paying customers, they think of a business more like a community group—that is, that customers give them money in order for them to create a community inside their office.

This perspective will kill a business. Fast.

I'm all for a great work community (without it, your team will suffer morale issues), but a business must succeed financially or the community will no longer exist. Add to this fact that if you do not understand how a business really works it could cost you a promotion or a raise in salary. And if you own or run a business, not understanding how a business really works could cost you everything. A business will sink or swim based on its team members making solid, wise decisions.

So, how does a business really work? If you know the answer to this single question, you can start a business, run a business, sell a business, or fix a business. Understanding how a business really works increases your personal economic value on the open market.

Of course, every business is different, but they all share a few important components. If you understand those components, you understand how to make a business healthy and profitable.

In the next five business days, I'm going to take you through a framework that will teach you how a business really works. The framework is designed to identify the kinds of decisions that make a business grow.

Using the analogy of an airplane, I'll show you the parts of a business and how they fit together to make a healthy machine capable of lifting off the ground to travel far and fast.

If you've ever worked in a small division of a company and wondered where you fit in the machine, this framework will help. And once you can see both the whole and its parts, you'll better understand how to lead not only yourself and your division, but how to help others create and sustain a business that grows in revenue and profit.

DAY TWENTY-ONE
How to Create Strategy—Understand How a Business Really Works

A value-driven professional knows a business works like an airplane.

How do you know whether a business is going to crash or fly?

To answer that question, you first have to understand the dynamics of flight.

In the most simple terms, a business works like a commercial airplane.

For my analogy, I'll show you five distinct parts that have to work together in order for the plane to fly. Each part will represent an aspect of your business. And each part has to be kept in proportion or the business will crash.

The Body: Overhead

The body of the airplane is, of course, where you put the people and the cargo. This is the largest part of the airplane, but

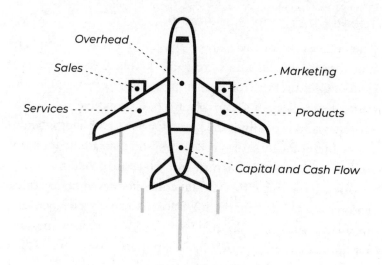

it's also the whole point of the airplane. The airplane exists to get people where they need to go. This is also why a business exists. A business exists to solve a problem for customers. In exchange for solving those problems, money is exchanged and team members get jobs, healthcare, and so on.

The body of the airplane represents your overhead. Overhead includes salaries, medical benefits, rent, office supplies, and so on. These are necessary expenses because it takes people and supplies to solve customers' problems in exchange for revenue.

The Wings: Products and Services

The wings of the airplane give it lift. When the engine thrusts the airplane forward, the air pressure lifts the wings off the ground, taking the body of the airplane with it.

Your products and services are what give a business lift. The wings of the airplane represent everything you sell. Think of the products you sell as the part of the plane that give the airplane lift. Without profitable products to sell, no air (revenue) can lift the airplane off the ground.

The Right Engine: Marketing

The engines thrust the plane forward. In a single-engine airplane, you'd likely only have a marketing budget, but in a dual-engine aircraft, you have a marketing budget and a sales team. Regardless, without some kind of engine selling the products and propelling the plane forward, the wings cannot create lift. Some kind of marketing system or sales team needs to thrust the business forward and sell those products.

Your marketing effort should come first, even before sales. The reason is—the marketing effort is usually cheaper, and until it exists, your sales team will not have a clear message out in the marketplace that backs up their efforts.

The Left Engine: Sales

It's true that a dual-engine plane can fly using only one of its engines, but when you fire the second engine up, the airplane moves with greater thrust and gets even more lift. It can now fly faster and farther and the body of the airplane can get even bigger, employing even more people to solve even more problems for customers.

Your second engine is your sales effort. Your sales team brings in even more money so the business can afford to grow and scale.

Fuel: Capital and Cash Flow

Lastly, the airplane will need fuel. No matter how efficient the airplane is or how light it is, without fuel it will crash. Fuel represents cash flow. A business may glide a little when it runs out of cash, but eventually it will crash and everybody onboard the body of the business will lose their livelihoods.

If you are growing a business, you may be using loans or working with investors, but the goal of any business is to eventually operate with a positive cash flow. Having enough cash to operate your business is, by far, the most important factor leading to business success.

How Do You Keep the Business Flying?

If the parts of an airplane are not in proportion to each other, the airplane will crash.

The right and left engine must produce enough thrust to move the plane forward, and the wings must be big enough to create lift. The body of the plane must be light enough to be lifted by the engine and the wings. And, of course, the plane must have enough fuel to stay in the air.

All of these principles are also true for a business. You must have a profitable product (or products) that customers want, and your marketing and sales efforts have to be strong enough to sell them. Additionally, you must keep overhead light so it doesn't bog the airplane down, and you have to have enough cash to pay bills.

So, how do you make good business decisions? Always remember the analogy of the airplane.

Whenever a business leader wants to increase overhead but can't connect that increased overhead to more or better products or stronger and more efficient sales efforts, they're asking to make the airplane heavier without increasing lift. That's a risky decision. All sections of the airplane must be kept in proportion. Always.

If you want to move the employees into a brand-new state-of-the-art office in an expensive part of town but do not have a successful line of products that are in demand by customers, you're making a terrible decision. Why? Because you're going to make the body of the airplane heavier without making the wings bigger or the engines stronger.

If you keep making decisions like that, the business will crash.

Based on the simple metaphor of the airplane, here are some things smart business leaders keep in mind as they run a company or a division of a company:

- **They are resistant to adding costs (especially recurring costs) to overhead.** Costs may make the body of the airplane too heavy and risk the job security of the entire workforce.
- **They get daily or weekly reports that reveal whether marketing and sales efforts are performing effectively.** They

make sure the left and right engines are producing sales to offset the cost of overhead.

- **They make sure the profit margins on the products they create are high enough to cover the overhead necessary to sell them.** They make sure every product covers the cost of itself and overhead, and that profit margins are high enough to provide job security for the entire team.
- **They are constantly increasing the efficiency of their production, sales, and marketing.** Good business leaders are obsessed with efficiency. Just like a good airplane engineer, business leaders are always trying to create a leaner, faster, more efficient machine. In other words, they make sure the activity-to-output ratios are high so that capital will go further.

Businesses get much more complicated as they grow, of course, but the five main parts of a business never change.

When you understand how a business works, you can quickly analyze what is and isn't working and monitor the health of the business.

Over the next five days, we are going to look at each part of the airplane in order to learn how to better run a business.

Once you understand how a business really works, you'll be able to make terrific decisions making your business, or the division of the business you work within, stronger and more efficient.

> ### Here's Today's Business Made Simple Tip of the Day
>
> Understand the five parts of a healthy business so you never experience a crash.

DAY TWENTY-TWO
How to Create Strategy—Keep Your Overhead Down

The body: Keep overhead as light as possible.

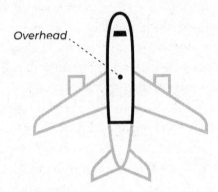

Overhead

When a business fails, it fails for one reason: Overhead got too high for sales to cover. In other words, the engines of the airplane were too weak and the wings on the airplane were too small to provide lift for the oversized body.

The principle of keeping overhead down seems quite obvious. Sadly, that most fundamental principle is often forgotten amid the day-to-day running of a business.

In the fog of a business year, a leader may approve an expensive research trip or bonus structure or double down on a failed product launch—and suddenly, cash flow hits zero.

And cash flow seems to always hit zero suddenly. Nobody seems to see it coming.

Failures like this are understandable. We all get so busy creating a product or imagining how great our marketing strategy is going to be that our overhead begins to expand when we aren't paying attention.

What is overhead?

There are many definitions for overhead, but this simple definition is one I've used for years: Overhead is anything involved in the cost of doing business that is not related to product creation, marketing, or sales.

In other words, overhead is anything that is not actively involved in creating thrust that moves the business forward or the wings that give it lift.

Overhead is rent, healthcare, sodas in the fridge at the office, and light bulbs blinking over that fridge. Overhead is the salary for any position that is not creating a product, marketing that product, or selling that product.

This is why, much to their chagrin, administrative team members are often paid less than those who make, market, or sell products.

Unless money is spent in the direct effort to make more money, that expenditure should be questioned. This is the key to keeping overhead in check.

This does not mean we get to spend as much money on marketing, sales, and product creation as we want. The truth is, we have to be lean, light, and efficient everywhere. That said, an expense that leads directly to greater lift is going to get approved much faster than an expense that adds only to the weight of the airplane.

It goes without saying that if your overhead (airplane body) gets big and heavy but your product offering is too limited (wings are too small) and your sales and marketing efforts are not strong (weak engines), the plane is going to crash.

We have to understand this principle if we want our business to succeed.

One way to make sure your product or business does not crash is to monitor the creeping expense of overhead.

For instance, when deciding whether or not to launch a product, a value-driven business leader will always want to know how that effort is going to affect overhead. Why? Because even though they are launching a product (making the wings larger), the overhead will almost certainly increase (the body will get larger) and they will want to calculate whether the larger wings will provide enough lift for the necessarily heavier body.

Before a pilot takes off, they do a careful calculation to make sure the plane is not too heavy. If the plane is small, in fact, sometimes bags and even customers will be removed from the plane to ensure the plane's safety.

A smart leader is going to make sure that the wings of the airplane are large, both engines are strong, and the body of the airplane is lean and light because they know, if they don't, the business will crash.

Again, the point is this: Keeping overhead down is always a priority. Otherwise, the business will get too heavy and it will crash.

Here are some questions a smart business strategist will ask in order to keep the business lean, light, and safe.

1. *Whose time is going to be taken up to create, launch, and sell this product?* Time is expensive. If we fail to calculate how much of our people's time is going to be taken up if we launch a product, we risk the security of the business.

2. *What new people need to be hired to run this project and what will they need to be paid?* Salaries are usually our largest expense and we need to know in advance how much this expense is going to grow because we've launched this product. Not only this, but we need to know how these salaries are divided into product creation, sales, and marketing versus administrative. Remember, product creation, sales, and marketing contribute to lift while much of administrative is necessary overhead.

3. *How much will our overhead increase if we launch this product?* Will we need a larger office, more healthcare, a larger HR department, further learning and development efforts, and so on? In other words, if we make the wings of the airplane larger, how much larger will the body need to be to support those wings?

4. *Are their unnecessary costs we can cut in this launch to make sure the entire plane doesn't get too heavy?* If we want the airplane to be safe and reliable, we must increase the efficiency and thrust of the engines, increase the size and strength of the wings, and decrease the weight of the body. In other words, we must increase efficiency everywhere. Always.

Here's Today's Business Made Simple Tip of the Day

In order to create a safe business that grows, categorize your expenses into four major categories: product creation, sales, marketing, and overhead.

DAY TWENTY-THREE
How to Create Strategy—Make and Sell the Right Products

Wings: Is there a demand for the products we are selling and are they profitable?

It's easy to get confused about what products we should create and which products we should allocate valuable sales resources to.

Often, these are emotional decisions. We love the team that wants to create "X" product, and to be honest, we owe them a

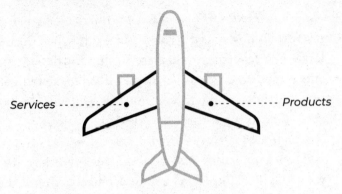

Services ------- • ------- Products

favor. Or, we doubled down on the importance of creating product "Y" in the last leadership meeting, and even though sales are low, we've got to chase that decision with further resources or we will look like we made a bad decision. Or worse, we have an opportunity to generate quick revenue if we put a little focus on product "Z" and God knows we need to pay bills.

None of these are good reasons to create a product or allocate valuable sales and marketing resources to that product.

The products you create are the wings of the airplane. When we sell those products, the airplane gets lift and allows us to fly.

When choosing what products to focus on, you want to choose products that have two critical characteristics:

1. **They are light.**
2. **They are strong.**

What do I mean by light and strong?

1. **They are light.** They can be sold for considerable profit or a smaller profit but at volume.
2. **They are strong.** There is a strong demand for the product in the marketplace.

In other words, regardless of how we feel about a product, we will only invest in products that are profitable and in demand. That's it. If we don't, we are strapping small, weak wings to our airplane and that will lead to a crash.

When deciding whether or not to create a product, sell a product, or even buy out a company that makes a product, profitability and demand are the most important considerations. Again, if a product is not in demand or profitable, the wings of your airplane will be flimsy and weak. They will not support the overhead of the aircraft and it will crash.

These criteria are also important for streamlining your product offering. Years ago, the company may have needed cash and decided to sell "X" product for $500. The cash flow improved for a moment until suddenly you were back where you started. Why? Because the product cost $425 to produce and the $75 profit wasn't enough to cover overhead.

That product wasn't light. It didn't have a good enough profit margin.

Another product may have been created because one customer said you really should bring it to market. They promised they'd buy it. So you spent a great deal of capital bringing it to market only to realize there was only one person in the world who wanted it. There was actually no other demand.

This was a bad decision, not because the product wasn't profitable, but because the demand was not high.

Based on these criteria, perhaps it's time to clean house at whatever company you manage. Are there products you are currently selling that are not profitable? Are there products you are warehousing that clearly are no longer in demand?

You can quickly strengthen the wings of your airplane by clearing out products that are not profitable or in demand and replacing them with products that are both.

Certain products are, of course, loss leaders—meaning you sell a lot of them at cost or below cost so you can upsell other items later. If that's the case, that product gets a pass.

But be careful. A better strategy would be to create products that lead to upsells that are also in demand and profitable.

Analyze the products you are selling. Are they strong and light? Is there a demand? Are they profitable?

If not, streamline your product offering so you aren't wasting precious overhead and energy pushing products that do not support the lift of the aircraft.

To be safe and airworthy, wings should be strong and light. In a business, products should be in demand and highly profitable.

> **Here's Today's Business Made Simple Tip of the Day**
>
> To increase revenue and profit in your business, analyze whether or not the products you are selling are in demand and profitable.

DAY TWENTY-FOUR
How to Create Strategy—Prioritize Marketing

Right engine/marketing: Test how you're going to market the product.

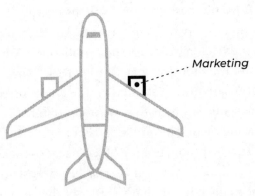

Marketing

One of my favorite movies of all time is *Field of Dreams*. In the movie, Kevin Costner plays a farmer told by a mysterious voice to build a baseball diamond in his cornfield. The voice whispers, over and over, *If you build it, they will come*. In the movie, he builds it, and they do.

As far as I know, that fictional movie is the only example of a thing that attracted attention just because it got built. Sadly, nearly everything else in life has to be built, then supported with a marketing campaign.

Here's a rule: If you don't attract people to the thing you built, they won't come.

If you think your business will thrive simply because you have a great product, you're wrong. There are simply too many great products out there. Companies that thrive are companies that master the art of telling customers about their products.

Later in this book, I will spend an entire week talking about how to build a successful marketing campaign, but for now let me give you a simple tip so you can know how to test a product to see if a marketing campaign will even work. Here it is:

Before launching a product, I ask the marketing department to build a landing page (marketing page) for that product so I can survey interest in the product itself.

I literally have a website built as though the product exists and then survey potential customers to query interest. Instead of placing a "buy now" button on the website, I'll place a "join the waitlist" button to see how many people click the button.

I'm not just talking about a wire-framed landing page on paper; I'm talking about an actual, hidden page on the web that looks exactly like the page we would build if the product already existed.

Building the marketing collateral before the product even exists does two things:

1. **Helps you clarify your marketing language.** Building the sales page for the product helps you create and review language that will pique a customer's interest. Build the page, talk about it as a staff, and share the page with a select group of potential customers to get feedback.
2. **Confirms consumer interest.** Once you've clarified your marketing language, you can release the page to the public or to a select group of customers for preorders. Collecting preorders is a great way to build excitement about the product and find out whether or not people are interested in the first place.

Your landing page is a rough draft, of course, but it should be created as though you are launching the product to market. Every detail should be considered.

Testing your marketing language is like testing an engine before you connect it to the body of the plane. Most businesses will wait till the last minute to prepare their marketing ideas because their energy is being used to create the product. But without the right marketing language and plan, nobody will be attracted to the product after it gets built. So why not test the engine first?

By creating a test sales page in advance, you will gain more confidence in how you talk about the product and whether or not it will be successful going to market. You will also cause your marketing team (or plan) to be ready well in advance of the launch so you're not waiting till the last minute to make sure this critical engine will provide thrust for the plane.

Of course, you want to make sure that the product can actually be built before you presell it to customers. That said, there are times that orders are so low, refunds must be given and the product launch should be canceled; otherwise, you risk crashing the airplane.

Again, later in this book, we will spend an entire week talking about how to create a marketing plan that works. For now, though, consider testing products before you release them as a way of protecting yourself from making dangerous mistakes.

> ### Here's Today's Business Made Simple Tip of the Day
>
> Create a marketing sales page to test marketing language and gauge interest in a product even before that product exists.

DAY TWENTY-FIVE
How to Create Strategy—Run a Sales System

Left engine/sales: Create a step-by-step path your customers can take to make a purchase, and monitor the progress of every lead.

In order for the sales engine of our business to produce thrust, we are going to need a sales framework and system.

It's not enough to just hire a salesperson and set them free. That salesperson needs a path to take customers down and personal accountability if they are going to excel.

Later, we will spend a full week in this book learning the Sales Made Simple framework, but for now, ask yourself how much more you, your salesperson, or your entire sales team would produce if they had a step-by-step path they could guide customers down along with metrics allowing them to know which customers were in which stages of the buying journey.

The point, of course, is to close more business. Weekly and monthly goals should be established that motivate sales professionals to guide more customers down the path.

Here's how your sales department should operate:

A Step-by-Step Path

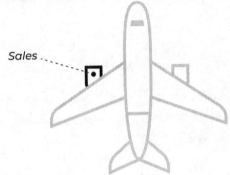

Sales

Every sales team needs a series of steps to take a qualified lead down in order to close a deal. That series of steps could look as simple as:

1. Qualify the lead.
2. Send the lead information and schedule a call.
3. Engage in an intake meeting.
4. Send a proposal highlighting predetermined talking points.
5. Enter into the closing sequence.

There are many ways to structure the path, but simply having a path will allow you to set goals and monitor the progress of every single lead. Again, later in this book, I will detail the Sales Made Simple framework that will provide an easy step-by-step path, but the point is to predetermine the path you want to take customers down and be able to count the number of leads at each stage of the path.

There are various software tools you can use to monitor which potential clients are at which stage of the relationship.

The point is this: When you create a step-by-step path for interacting with potential clients, you know more about the customers' needs and so enter into more meaningful relationships, help more customers solve their problems, and close more sales.

Do you have a step-by-step path you guide customers down in order to close a sale? And do you know which phase each customer is in so you can interact with them in the most helpful manner possible? If not, create a sales system and serve more customers while increasing overall revenue.

> ### Here's Today's Business Made Simple Tip of the Day
>
> Increase sales by creating a step-by-step path your customers can take. Then monitor the progress of every lead.

DAY TWENTY-SIX
How to Create Strategy—Protect Cash Flow

Fuel: Watch cash flow closely because if you run out of cash, the business will crash.

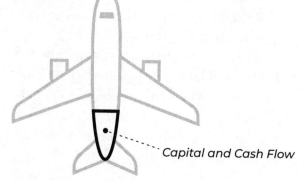

Capital and Cash Flow

You can have a perfectly sound airplane with giant, strong wings, a lean, light body, and two powerful engines and yet still suffer a horrific crash if you run out of fuel.

In a business, accessible money in the bank is fuel. If you don't have a strong cash flow, the plane will crash no matter what.

In every decision we make, it is important to ask ourselves how this decision will affect cash flow. If a new product is going to take an enormous amount of research and development followed by expensive production and a long sales cycle, we are essentially deciding to fly into a headwind that is going to drain fuel fast. That decision needs to be made carefully.

A shocking number of business leaders go with their gut on whether or not they have the capital to fuel whatever project they want to embark on. But a good pilot would never trust their gut on whether they have enough fuel.

In fact, anybody who's taken a couple of flying lessons knows that, before taking off, you don't even trust your fuel gauge. You literally crawl up on the wing and use an instrument to make sure, physically, that there is fuel in those tanks.

Here are seven financial questions to ask before making an important business decision:

1. How much cash will we need to create this product before we launch it?
2. What is our profit margin on this product? Will it be able to return cash to the coffers?
3. When will we start making money on this product?
4. How will launching this product affect our other revenue streams? Will it reduce cash coming in from somewhere else?
5. Does losing money on this product generate sales and profits elsewhere? If so, how much?

6. How can we make this product more profitable?
7. What iterations of this product could we sell for more money?

Use these questions to stimulate thought regarding each of your revenue streams. Make sure you use the questions to generate actual numbers. Until you get to actual numbers, you're only hoping you have enough fuel. Actual numbers will tell you whether you can make the journey or not. Numbers don't lie.

Nothing sends up a red flag for your boss faster than a conversation in which it becomes obvious that you don't understand cash flow. Decisions should be made based solely on their ability to directly or indirectly affect the amount of cash coming into the company.

I call this line of thinking the "fuel filter," because every decision has to be filtered through the question "how will this affect cash?"

Do you run every decision through the fuel filter, asking how this decision will affect the company's ability to maintain a healthy cash flow?

Here's Today's Business Made Simple Tip of the Day

In every decision you make, ask yourself how the decision will affect cash flow.

A Value-Driven Professional

* *Increase your personal economic value by mastering each core competency.*

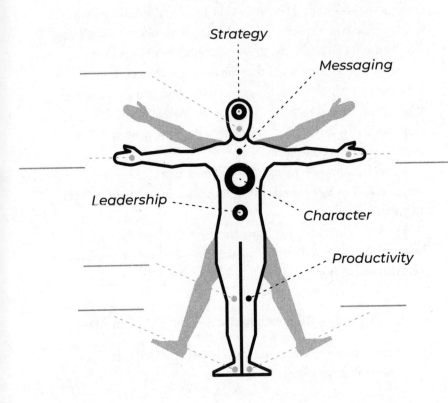

CHAPTER FIVE

MESSAGING MADE SIMPLE

How (and Why) to Clarify Your Marketing Message

INTRODUCTION

Now that we've established the character of a competent professional, learned to cast a vision, become more personally productive, and arrived at an understanding of how a business really works, it's time to learn how to clarify a message.

All of those projects we are working on won't go anywhere unless we can explain their importance to customers in a marketing message that attracts buyers.

Customers are not only attracted to a good product, they are attracted to a clear message that describes that product.

In the next two sections of the book, I'm going to teach you how to clarify a marketing message and then create a sales funnel using the sound bites you generate from that clarification process.

Any professional who knows how to clarify a marketing message is worth thousands more in the marketplace. Why? Because a clear message sells product.

The hardest thing to do as a professional is to get people's attention, but in the next five days I'm going to teach you how. I'm going to teach you to invite customers into a clear, compelling message.

If you can clearly explain what sort of better life people get when they buy your product, you will sell more products.

In the next five days, I'm going to teach you how to create several strategic sound bites that make customers want to buy your products.

Once you have your sound bites down, you can repeat them over and over as though you are taking the world through an exercise in memorization. That's what disciplined marketers do. They take the world through an exercise in memorization. Amateurs speak their minds, but value-driven professionals guide people's thoughts by repeating disciplined sound bites that invite customers to buy a product that will change their lives for the better.

When your sound bites are created, you can write them down into the framework in Figure 5.1.

The grid will make more sense after you experience the next five days. You can create a messaging grid of your own

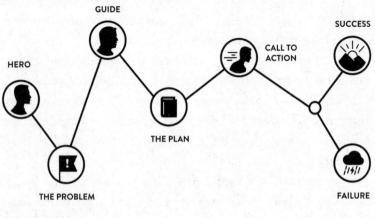

FIGURE 5.1

using a tool I created at MyStoryBrand.com. That tool is also free.

Once you understand how to clarify a message, you can use that message to create marketing collateral, give better speeches, design a terrific elevator pitch, or even tell the story of why your work matters to the world. In short, once you create a clear message, you can positively impact the world through your business.

Can you clearly state how your products change people's lives? Do you have sound bites that make people want to know more, or even make a purchase? When you try to wire-frame a website or write a speech, do you feel stuck?

In the next five days, I'll introduce you to the StoryBrand messaging framework that will help you clarify your message, so people actually listen.

DAY TWENTY-SEVEN
How to Clarify Your Message—Use Story to Engage Customers

When clarifying your message, use the power of story.

The average person spends 30 percent of their time daydreaming. In fact, much of the time we are talking with others, listening to speeches, scrolling through our phones, and even eating a meal, we are completely checked out.

Daydreaming and checking out aren't bad things. In fact, daydreaming is a survival mechanism. When we daydream, we're conserving mental energy in case we need it later for survival. Literally, if something isn't interesting, your mind will put you in daydream mode so you don't use the energy you might need later if you encounter a threat.

Sadly, this means most of the time we are trying to explain something important to somebody, they're fighting the temptation to daydream.

Unless.

The only tool known to man that can stop people from daydreaming is story. When we start to hear a story, we stop daydreaming and pay attention.

Story is that powerful.

Most people, though, don't know how to tell a story and certainly don't know how to filter their message through the ancient elements of story in order to get people's attention.

For you, that changes today. I'm going to teach you a formula for telling a story and then spend the next week unpacking that formula so you can create great marketing messages, give terrific presentations, and command attention.

Here we go . . .

A Character That Wants Something: A good story starts with a character. A character comes on the screen and within minutes we have to know what that character wants. Whatever the character wants has to be clearly defined. He has to want to marry the woman. She has to want to disarm the bomb. Whatever it is, it has to be specific or we will lose the audience.

The Character Encounters a Problem: Next, we can't let the character get what they want or the story won't be interesting. We've got to define some kind of problem the character is struggling with. The problem is the key. If we don't define the problem, people will stop paying attention.

The Character Meets the Guide: Next, our hero meets another character called the guide who has overcome the same problem the hero is dealing with. The guide then helps the hero overcome their problem and win the day.

The Guide Gives the Hero a Plan: Then, the guide gives the hero a plan they can use to overcome their problem. Usually this plan unfolds in a series of steps that defines the journey the hero has to take to win the day.

The Guide Calls the Hero to Action: After laying out the plan, the guide challenges the hero to take action. They must make a move toward solving their problem and overcoming their challenge. Heroes don't take action unless they are challenged by the guide to do so.

Define the Stakes—Success: Once the hero takes action, there must be stakes in the story or it gets boring. What will life look like if the hero wins the day? Will he marry the girl? Will she save the village? The storyteller must paint a picture of what life looks like if everything goes well.

Define the Stakes—Failure: It is equally important to let the audience know what life will look like for the hero if they do not win the day. Will the hero be lonely forever? Will the village suffer loss of life? If nothing bad can happen to our hero, the story is dull and boring. Something must be potentially won or lost or the story won't engage the audience.

Whenever you are giving a presentation (I'll share more tips on giving presentations in a later section of this book), or wire-framing a website, or even giving an elevator pitch, use this simple story formula to engage your audience.

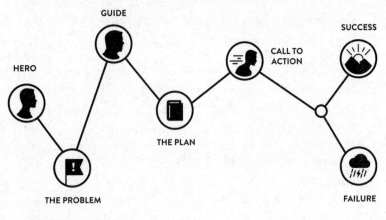

FIGURE 5.1

For instance, here is the story formula used by a baker to sell a wedding cake:

A Character That Wants Something: Every bride wants a beautiful wedding cake that reflects the meaning of the moment.

The Character Encounters a Problem: The problem is that most wedding cakes taste terrible and literally leave a bad taste in the guests' mouths.

The Character Meets the Guide: At Eighth Street Bakery, we got tired of bad-tasting wedding cakes and developed a process in which gorgeous wedding cakes can actually taste fantastic.

The Guide Gives the Hero a Plan: To work with us, simply make an appointment, come by the shop for a taste testing, and schedule your cake for delivery.

The Guide Calls the Hero to Action: Schedule your appointment today.

Define the Stakes—Success: If you do, your guests will be astonished at the beauty of your cake and keep coming back for seconds.

Define the Stakes—Failure: Don't let your cake be a bad-tasting letdown. Schedule an appointment today.

Now that's a sales pitch. And that language can be used in presentations, marketing websites, emails, and even in a video.

Once you know how story works, you can clarify any message so people will listen.

In the next four days, we will take a closer look at these elements of story and help you craft a clearer and clearer message. No matter what project you're working on, being able to talk about it in an engaging way will attract the resources you need to make the project a success.

Here's Today's Business Made Simple Tip of the Day

Know how to filter your marketing message through the elements of a story in order to engage an audience.

DAY TWENTY-EIGHT
How to Clarify Your Message—Position Your Customer as the Hero

When clarifying your marketing message, never position yourself as the hero. Always position yourself as the guide.

In stories, heroes are not the strongest character. In fact, heroes are often unwilling to take action, filled with self-doubt, worried the story won't turn out well, and in desperate need of help.

In stories, heroes are weak characters becoming strong.

There is another character in most stories, though, who is already strong. The guide exists in the story to help the hero win. For this reason, whenever we clarify our message, we want to position ourselves as the guide, not the hero.

It's great to play the hero in life. In fact, we are all heroes on a mission trying to accomplish something. But in business, switch rolls and play the guide. Guides exist to help heroes win, and that's why businesses exist. They exist to solve customers' problems, help them win, and transform them into better (or more equipped) versions of their prior selves.

An average person wears many hats every day. In the morning, while reviewing their life plan and planning the day, they play the hero. Then, while helping their kids get ready for school, they put on the guide hat, helping their kids become their best selves.

Later, at the office, they continue playing the hero as they tackle their daily tasks. But as soon as they pick up the phone to talk to a customer, they switch into the guide.

To accomplish much in life, play the hero, but when with customers, always play the guide and never play the hero. Why? Because customers are looking for a guide who can help them win the day. They aren't looking for another hero.

Some of our favorite characters in movies are actually the guides. In *Star Wars*, Yoda and Obi-Wan help Luke and his friends fight the evil empire. And in *The Hunger Games*, Haymitch helps Katniss survive and win the day.

Guides are the strongest characters in the story because they have already overcome the very same challenges the heroes must now overcome. That means they are experienced and equipped and know how to win.

In life, people in need (which at times is all of us) do not look around for other heroes; we look around for guides. So, if a brand, product, or leader positions itself as the hero and not the guide, customers will often look past it for another brand, leader, or product.

What's the difference between positioning as the hero and positioning as the guide? A hero tells their own story while a guide understands the hero story and sacrifices to help them win.

Guides are strong, self-assured, and know how to defeat the villain. Guides counsel the hero on their journey.

Position your brand, your project, or yourself as the guide and people will follow your lead.

How do you position yourself as the guide? Here are the two characteristics of a competent guide:

1. **Empathy.** The guide understands the hero's challenge and identifies with their pain. They care about the hero.
2. **Authority.** The guide is competent to help the hero solve their problem. The guide knows what they are doing.

The one-two punch in communication as a professional is to say *I know what you're struggling with and I can help you get out of it.*

When you are clarifying your message in order to create marketing material, give a speech, an elevator pitch, or even during a meeting, play the guide by being empathetic to your audience's problems and being competent to get them through those problems.

Here's Today's Business Made Simple Tip of the Day

When clarifying your message, position yourself, your products, and your brand as the guide, not the hero.

DAY TWENTY-NINE
How to Clarify Your Message—Talk about Your Customer's Problem

When clarifying your marketing message, know the problem is the hook.

A story doesn't really get going until the main character encounters a problem. You can tell us the character's name, where they live, who they hang out with, and what they want, but until a problem shows up that challenges the character, an audience will wonder when the story is going to get started.

So, how does this story truth translate into business?

It means this: Until you start talking about your product, or your brand as the solution to somebody's problem, they won't be interested.

The problem is the hook. Until the storyteller introduces the challenge the main character is up against, the audience sits wondering what the story is about.

Think about it. Is isn't till we understand that Jason Bourne has no idea who he is that the movie gets interesting. And if Frodo Baggins could have destroyed the ring simply by tossing it in the trash in his little kitchen, we wouldn't have a story. The entire story is about the hero overcoming *conflict*. Why? Because conflict is what an audience pays attention to.

What does this mean for our marketing message? It means that we have to keep talking about our customers' problems or they won't be interested in our products.

If you're creating some talking points about a product, make sure to define the exact problem your product resolves. What pain are you taking away? What roadblock are you removing? What villain are you defeating? Ask yourself these questions and the answer will reveal why your product is worth purchasing.

The more you talk about the problem you solve, the more value you attribute to your product or service.

Sadly, when clarifying their message, most professionals tell their story. They talk about how their grandfather started the company and how long they've been in business. But these are wasted words. The very first thing any professional should talk about is the problem they or their product can solve. Until they talk about the problem, people are wondering whether they should even listen.

What problem do you solve? What problem does the division of the company you work within solve? What problem does your product solve? Define this problem and people will finally start to listen.

Here's Today's Business Made Simple Tip of the Day

When clarifying your marketing message, define the problem you solve.

DAY THIRTY
How to Clarify Your Message—Create a Clear Call to Action

When clarifying your marketing message, define what action you want your audience to take.

A clear message inspires action.

A clear message does not change the world. The action people take after hearing a clear message changes the world.

The world that we know was not built by people sitting around looking at their belly buttons; it was built by people who were inspired to take action.

During World War II, soldiers on the British front lines were only inspired to fight by the weekly address from their prime minister, Winston Churchill. After watching friends get killed and having hope diminished, it was the weekly messages of Winston Churchill and his calls to action that kept them going.

In a good story, the guide must confidently ask the hero to take action or the hero will lose confidence and fail.

Why? Because when the guide fails to confidently ask people to take action, the listener begins to doubt the guide's competence. Can you or can't you get the hero out of this predicament?

Obi-Wan Kenobi cannot politely suggest that Luke *use the force as a potential option*; he must declare a clear direction that Luke will "use the force."

Audiences can smell whether or not you believe in your ideas or your products. You either have a solution or you do not. You are either confident or you are not. You can either help in their journey or you cannot. If you cannot, you will politely ask them to buy your product in such a way that you sound like you're asking for charity (because you are). If you can help them, though, you will tell them to buy your product or use your service because you no longer want them to struggle with their problem.

Many professionals do not understand the power of competence and confidence. If you actually have a solution to people's problems, and you have the confidence to invite people into that solution, you should stand in that confidence.

The truth is, if you confidently tell people what they need to do to solve a problem, they will do it, but if you sheepishly suggest what people can do to solve the problem, they most likely won't.

Years ago, I was teaching a StoryBrand messaging workshop to about two hundred business leaders. I come alive in a classroom. I was honestly designed to be a professor and I love finding ways to make a point without using a textbook or a PowerPoint slide. I told the audience I had a very important point to make, only I was going to make it on the sidewalk outside the building.

I asked the group to stand up and follow me out the door.

All two hundred business leaders got up slowly, somewhat confused, and walked out the door, through the lobby, and onto the curb by the street. I then stood up on a box, grabbed a bullhorn, and told them the very important point I wanted to make.

I said to the crowd on the curb: "Always remember this. *People will go where you tell them to go.*"

The class laughed and shook their heads and then we slowly went back into the building.

Here was the real point I wanted my class to understand: If you do not tell people what to do, they will not do anything. If you don't end a speech with a clear call to action, people will not take action. If you do not give people step-by-step instructions on your website, they will not take a step at all.

As you create the talking points that make up your clear message, include a strong call to action; otherwise, you will never change the world.

Here's Today's Business Made Simple Tip of the Day

When clarifying your message, include a strong call to action.

DAY THIRTY-ONE
How to Clarify Your Message—Define the Stakes and Create Urgency

When clarifying your message, be sure to define what's at stake.

When I was a kid, my mother used to take my sister and me to the dollar theater on Friday night. She'd pay a dollar for each of us, and then another dollar for popcorn and a Coke. Mind you, we were poor, and going to the theater was a big deal.

I swear to you, though, I would not trade growing up rich for those experiences. They were nearly magical.

It was in that dollar theater that I fell in love with stories. Of course we were seeing those movies a couple months behind the rich families, but who cares. The movies were amazing. Would Elliot get E.T. back home? Would Luke destroy the Death Star? Would Rocky defeat Apollo Creed?

I had some terrific experiences sitting in that theater as a kid. Those experiences would later cause me to study stories, to write books and a screenplay of my own, and much later to help more than a few leaders craft messages that matter.

So, what made all those stories so great? Well, the same thing that had me standing on my seat throwing popcorn into the air at the end of *The Karate Kid* when I was twelve years old is the same thing that will help you invite customers into a great story: the stakes. Could Daniel really beat the bully and win the karate tournament with a hurt leg? It turned out he could.

Do you want people as engaged in you and your brand as I was in *The Karate Kid*? Do you want to differentiate yourself as a leader? Do you want your product to matter on the open market? Do you want your brand to stand out in a crowded segment? If you do, define what's at stake if the audience chooses somebody else over you.

If you don't define what's at stake, you will fade from memory faster than one of those black-and-white German films that chooses to be artful rather than interesting.

What's at stake if we do or do not buy your product? What can be won or lost if we choose another brand over yours?

If there are no stakes, there is no story.

Spend some time answering these questions:

1. What will people's lives look like if they engage the story I'm inviting them into?
2. What will people's lives look like if they don't engage in the story I'm inviting them into?

Define what's at stake and your story will get very, very interesting.

Here's Today's Business Made Simple Tip of the Day

When clarifying your marketing message, define what can be won or lost if people don't engage in the story you're inviting them into.

A Value-Driven Professional

* *Increase your personal economic value by mastering each core competency.*

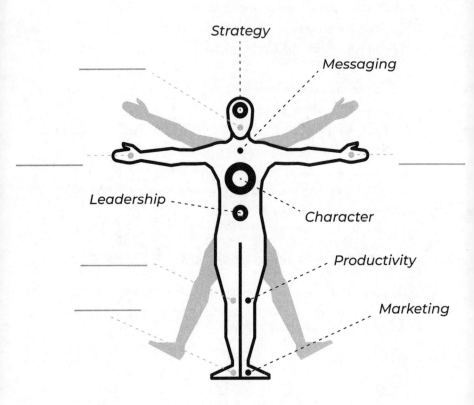

CHAPTER SIX

MARKETING MADE SIMPLE

How to Create a Sales Funnel That Converts Potential Customers into Buyers

INTRODUCTION

Having established the character of a competent professional, learned to unite a team around a vision, increased our personal productivity, come to understand how to keep a business from crashing, and learned to clarify a marketing message, it's time to become a marketing expert.

Not every professional works in the marketing department, but every professional needs to know enough about marketing that they can get word out about their ideas, products, and initiatives.

Marketing isn't just about delivering messages to customers, it's also about delivering messages to coworkers, stakeholders, and even the press or media.

At Business Made Simple, we teach our students a basic marketing methodology called a sales funnel. A sales funnel is one of the simplest, most inexpensive, and yet effective marketing strategies you can implement. In fact, I consider a sales funnel to be the foundation of any good marketing plan.

Sales funnels can be used to engage customers or they can be used for internal communication. They can be used for B2C or B2B communication. They can be used in for-profit or nonprofit endeavors. It hardly matters. A sales funnel works.

In fact, in March of 2020 when a novel coronavirus shut down the global economy and most retail businesses shut their doors for months, I noticed that businesses with a sales funnel were much more likely to survive. Why? Because of the two things that a sales funnel does for you:

1. It earns trust and familiarity with customers.
2. It allows you to reach out to them and pivot your message.

The reason they were able to survive is because businesses who had built sales funnels had collected email addresses and contact information. They were then able to pivot their message and their offerings to reflect the crisis. Businesses who didn't have sales funnels were not able to reach out to their customers and so were forgotten.

If you're growing a business, a sales funnel should be the first thing you create in your marketing plan.

For the next five days, I'll introduce you to the Marketing Made Simple methodology and will reveal to you the five parts of a sales funnel.

While most marketing training is philosophical, this training is intended to be pragmatic. We want you to be able to build or supervise the build of basic marketing tools that have been proven to get results.

Regardless of whether you will ever be a professional marketer, understanding what a sales funnel is and how it works dramatically increases your value on the open market. Everybody should understand how to tell people what they do and why it matters.

Not only this, but when you're done with this week's readings and videos, you'll know more about marketing than 95 percent of business leaders. That puts you in an elite group of professionals who are able to deliver exceptional value to any organization.

DAY THIRTY-TWO
How to Create a Marketing Campaign—
Understand a Sales Funnel

A great marketer knows how to build a sales funnel.

All sales are relational. People hear commercial messages about products and services all the time, but they mostly discard the information. That is, unless they hear about products and services from people or brands they trust.

To understand how to create a marketing plan that works, then, we have to understand how relationships work.

All relationships move through three stages (see Figure 6.1).

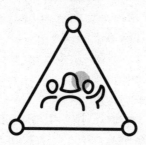

CURIOSITY

COMMITMENT   ENLIGHTENMENT

FIGURE 6.1

When people first meet us, they are either curious to know more about us or they are not. The same is true with brands and with products. People either want to know more or they don't. And, sometimes, it takes a few times of seeing your brand before people are willing to engage.

But what makes somebody want to know more?

Curiosity

Whether people are curious about you or your brand depends on whether they can associate you with their survival.

I know that sounds primitive, but it's true. Human beings are designed to survive and are constantly running data they encounter through a mental filter. Can this product help me survive and thrive? Will a relationship with this person help me feel safer or give me more resources so I can more easily succeed in the world?

Let's say we're at a party and somebody piques our curiosity (triggers our survival radar). If we're young and single, this person may be attractive, so our survival filter is triggered by the idea we may have found a companion. Or let's say we're older and this person went to a conference we're thinking about going to, so they triggered our survival filter by having information about whether or not we should spend our resources to go. Whatever it is that made us curious, I assure you it was about survival of some sort.

In order to pique somebody's curiosity, then, we have to associate our products or services with their survival.

Survival can be anything from saving money, making money, meeting new people, learning more healthy recipes, experiencing much-needed rest, gaining status, and more. Nearly any product or service can be associated with the customer's survival.

Piquing somebody's curiosity by associating ourselves or our products and services with their survival is how we earn the right to move into the next phase of relationships: enlightenment.

Enlightenment

After piquing your customers' curiosity, it's time to enlighten them about whether or not we really can help them survive.

Enlightening a customer about how your product can help them survive simply means telling them how. How does this product work to help me survive? How much better will my life look if I use this product? What have other people said about this product?

After customers get interested in our product because we made them curious, we can slow down our communication a little and enlighten them about how the product works.

Only after a person is enlightened and convinced their problem can be solved and their survival will be enhanced are they willing to move on to the next stage of a relationship: commitment.

Commitment

A commitment happens in a relationship when a person is willing to take a risk on another person or a product they believe will help them survive.

If we're talking about a product or service, a commitment simply means the customer is willing to give their money in exchange for the item they believe will help them survive.

Commitment happens when a customer places an order.

Sadly, most marketing efforts do not follow the natural progression of relationships and so they fail.

Relationships take time. If we ask for a commitment before we pique somebody's curiosity or enlighten them about our product, they will walk away. We must slowly, over time, pique our customer's curiosity, enlighten them about our product, and then ask them for a commitment.

The Marketing Made Simple sales funnel, which I'll introduce you to over the next four days, will build a relationship with your customer slowly and naturally so they are more likely to trust you and place an order.

See the parts of the Marketing Made Simple sales funnel in Figure 6.2.

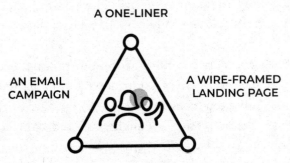

FIGURE 6.2

Once you know how to create a sales funnel, you will be able to execute a marketing plan that earns your customers' trust, builds strong relationships, and grows your brand.

Whether you want to build a sales funnel or not, knowing what a sales funnel includes and how it works will increase your value in any organization because you will know what the marketing plan that promotes your products or ideas should look like.

Here's Today's Business Made Simple Tip of the Day

Learn to create a sales funnel that works so you can build strong relationships with customers.

DAY THIRTY-THREE
How to Create a Marketing Campaign—Write a One-Liner That Generates Sales

A great marketer knows how to craft a one-liner.

The first step to creating a relationship with a customer is to pique their curiosity. But how can we do that in one, simple sentence?

When most people are asked what they do, they state the name of the company they work for or perhaps their job title.

This information fails to pique anybody's curiosity. But what if they answered the question differently? What if the way they answered the question made people ask for their business card or try to get on their schedule?

As I talked about in the introduction to this section, the key to piquing somebody's curiosity is to associate your product or service with their survival. And there's a foolproof formula for doing that.

To create one sentence that piques a customer's curiosity, create what we call a Marketing Made Simple one-liner.

The idea comes from the movie industry. Whenever a screenwriter writes a screenplay, they need to be able to summarize the story so producers want to invest and, eventually, if the movie gets made, people will want to go to the theater to see it.

When it comes to getting people to spend money on a movie, the one-sentence story summary can make or cost a movie studio hundreds of millions of dollars.

But what if a business had a one-liner? What if a business had one sentence (or a statement) that summarized the story their products invite people into and that sentence made people want to know more and perhaps even buy that product?

A Marketing Made Simple one-liner is that sentence. Your one-liner has three components:

1. A problem
2. Your product as a solution
3. The result

If you look at the structure of the one-liner, it's actually a short story. A character has a problem and finds a fix to solve it.

The result is that people lean in when you explain what you do.

For instance, if you were at a party and asked somebody what they did and they told you they were an "at-home chef" you'd likely have questions about how they got started or what their favorite restaurants were or if they'd ever cooked for anybody famous.

But if you met another at-home chef who was just as good and charged the same price, but when you asked what they did, said:

"You know how most families don't eat together and when they do they don't eat healthy? I'm an at-home chef. I cook in people's homes so they can eat well and spend more time with each other."

Now that at-home chef isn't just going to get more business; they are going to get all the business. Why? Because they piqued people's curiosity by inviting them into a story in which they are better positioned to survive and thrive. The customer is now wondering:

Will this work for me?
How much does it cost?
Do you cook once a week or every night?

The first chef stated their job description; the second chef stated a one-liner.

When people ask what you do, do you have one simple sentence or statement that piques their curiosity?

Once you've created your one-liner, print it on the back of your business card. Use your one-liner as your email signature. Make sure to include your one-liner on your website. Memorize your one-liner so that when people ask you what you do, you give a clear answer that grows your business.

Your one-liner is the closest thing you'll ever create to a magical sentence that causes people to want to do business with you.

> **Here's Today's Business Made Simple Tip of the Day**
>
> As the first element of your marketing plan, pique a customer's curiosity by creating a one-liner.

DAY THIRTY-FOUR
How to Create a Marketing Campaign—
Wire-Frame an Effective Website

A great marketer knows how to wire-frame a website that passes the grunt test.

The next element of the sales funnel you'll want to create is your website. There are many possible sections to an effective website, but there is one rule you must follow if you want your website to be as effective as possible: Your website must pass the grunt test.

Most people do not read websites, they scan them. In order for a person to stop scanning a website and start reading it—to move from curiosity to a desire for enlightenment—you must further pique their curiosity by clearly communicating the answer to three critical questions.

These questions are so primitive that even a caveman should be able to pull the answers from the bold, large text on your site.

Imagine handing a caveman a laptop that is open to your website and giving them five seconds to browse your landing page.

In only five seconds, would the caveman be able to clearly state the answer to these three questions:

1. What do you offer?
2. How will it make my life better?
3. What do I need to do to buy it?

If those three questions cannot be answered within five seconds of looking at your website, you're losing money.

Do you install swimming pools that will allow a family to enjoy the summer? And to have one installed, should I click the "get a quote" button? If a caveman can grunt what you offer, how it will make his life better, and what he needs to do to buy it after reviewing your site for as little as five seconds, congratulations, you've communicated clearly.

Most companies want to share far too much information on their website. The truth is, people don't need to know your grandmother started the company or that you won an award ten years ago from the Chamber of Commerce.

What they do need to know is what you offer, how it will make their lives better, and what they need to do to buy it.

The top section of your website is most important because it frames the rest of the message you'll present on the page. We call this section the header. If the header of your website passes the grunt test, you will see an increase in sales.

Here's Today's Business Made Simple Tip of the Day

As the second element of your marketing plan, learn to wire-frame a website that passes the grunt test.

DAY THIRTY-FIVE
How to Create a Marketing Campaign—Collect Email Addresses

A great marketer captures email addresses by offering free value.

Once you pique your customers' curiosity with your one-liner and your website, you can begin to enlighten them using a lead generator. Then, you further enlighten them through emails until you begin to ask for a commitment.

Most people are pretty good at the website part, but that's where their marketing campaign stops.

If you aren't collecting email addresses, I likely understand why. You don't want to bother somebody with a sales pitch. Or you don't know what you'd do with the email addresses once you got them. Or you don't know how all the technology works.

Those are all valid reasons, but none of them are strong enough to justify not collecting and sending emails. Email marketing is simply too inexpensive and too profitable for you to ignore.

If you're not collecting email addresses, you should be.

But how do we collect email addresses without being pushy or sleazy?

The key is to offer tangible, free value in exchange for a potential customer's contact information.

These days, psychologically, people consider the value of their email address at about ten or twenty dollars. That means they are only willing to give up their email address for something they would actually pay ten or twenty dollars for. That means in order for somebody to give up their email address, we need to offer them something they really want or need.

Thankfully, you are likely a subject expert in some realm that gives you information other people would find valuable. If you are a dentist, you might know five or six strategies that will help kids love to brush their teeth. Parents would love to read that. If you own a pet store, I bet you know how to get a dog to stop jumping on people when they walk through the door. Dog owners would likely find that information valuable.

When you offer free value in the form of a PDF or a series of videos in exchange for an email address, people are less likely to resent you emailing them after they download it. And besides, if they do, they can always unsubscribe from your emails.

The key here, though, is to offer something of great value. And that value should be specific and should solve a problem that your potential customers face.

You've likely tried to collect email addresses in the past by starting a newsletter, but nobody wants to subscribe to your newsletter. Why? Because they don't know what specific problem your newsletter solves. A PDF entitled "How to get your dog to stop jumping on people," on the other hand, offers clear value.

Whatever you offer, make sure the value is clear.

Here are some rules for creating something people will exchange for an email address:

1. **Make it short.** You don't have to write an entire book or film a full-length documentary.

2. **Give it a cover.** Dress it up so the outside looks like it has as much value as you've put on the inside. White papers don't collect very many email addresses.

3. **Make it solve a specific problem.** People will give their email addresses in exchange for something that lessens frustration or pain in their lives.

To enlighten your customers and further the chance they will make an eventual commitment, continue to build the relationship and earn trust with a lead generator that helps them solve a problem.

Here's Today's Business Made Simple Tip of the Day

As the third element of your marketing plan, create a lead generator that captures email addresses.

DAY THIRTY-SIX
How to Create a Marketing Campaign—
Email Your Customers

A great marketer builds relationships and closes the sale with an email campaign.

Years ago, when I first started dating my wife, she gave me the best marketing advice I've ever received. She said: "Don, you're a *quality* time guy, but I'm a *quantity* time girl."

She didn't mean it as marketing advice, actually. She meant it as dating advice. She was telling me how to win her heart. She didn't want to move fast. She wanted time.

Specifically, she knew I was the type of guy who knew what I wanted and had a strong bias toward action. But that wasn't going to work with her. What she wanted was for me to hang out long enough and in a variety of situations so that any weirdness would come out and she'd know what she was getting.

Smart woman.

It goes without saying that I slowed down. I moved to her town, rented a house in her neighborhood, and spent months sitting in her living room having tea with her and her girlfriends, my pinky pointed at the sky. It was a sacrifice, but I got the girl.

Years later, while analyzing some data and realizing our customers were not buying the first time they came to our website, or even after reading a lead generator they'd downloaded, but only after, months later, they'd received dozens of valuable emails containing valuable content, I had a significant epiphany: They're *quantity time* customers. They need to hear from us again and again before they will trust us. They're like Betsy.

Creating an email campaign gives you the chance to spend *quantity* time with your customers. Slowly, over a period of weeks, months, and perhaps even years, your customers become accustomed to hearing from you, receiving free value, and begin to trust you. Trust, of course, leads to commitment.

After downloading or watching your lead generator, customers should continue to receive incredible value from having given you their email address. You should continue to solve their problems, encourage them, inspire and inform them.

And, of course, you want to ask them to buy from you. Let them know about products that will help them solve their problems. Use every P.S. to repeat that offer and perhaps even offer a bonus.

Asking a customer for a commitment is a big deal. They could easily lose their money or even feel like a fool for making the wrong decision. We should not expect our customers to make those decisions without first having earned their trust.

After offering a lead generator, craft as many valuable emails as you can and stay in touch with your customers. Offer recipes, study guides, DIY tips, perspectives on ideas, whatever you think will serve your customers' concerns and interests.

When you stay in touch with your customers by sending them valuable emails, they trust you. And when they trust you, they commit and place orders.

Here's Today's Business Made Simple Tip of the Day

As the fourth element of your marketing plan, start an email campaign that earns your customers' trust and asks for their commitment.

A Value-Driven Professional

* *Increase your personal economic value by mastering each core competency.*

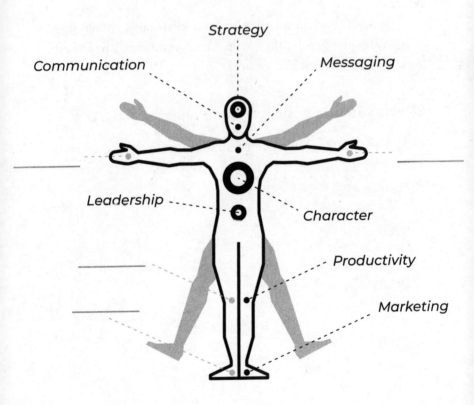

CHAPTER SEVEN

COMMUNICATION MADE SIMPLE

How to Become an Exceptional Communicator

INTRODUCTION

Having established the character of a competent professional, learned to unite a team around a mission, become more productive, learned how a business really works, clarified our message, and understood how to build a sales funnel, let's take some time to become excellent communicators. Let's learn to give a great presentation.

Whether you're leading a meeting, launching an initiative, giving a keynote address, or even hosting a webinar, any professional who can keep a room's attention while giving a speech is going to be given more responsibility and more pay. A good communicator is going to be chosen to lead.

Sadly, sitting through most corporate presentations can be torture. Slide after slide of data-driven bullet points is a great way to kill momentum on any important project.

Occasionally, though, you have the privilege of watching a presentation that informs and inspires. And you're not quite sure why. You just assume the person who gave the presentation is a great communicator. In fact, that's soon how she is described within the organization, as a great communicator.

But what is she doing that is so different? And can what she's doing be taught and learned?

The answer is yes. And the specifics about what she's doing will surprise you. It turns out that she's doing a few little things that hook the audience from the beginning and keep them interested right up until she's done.

So, what does a great communicator do that other communicators don't?

This is important because in order to be given more and more responsibility, we have to be able to deliver a presentation that captivates people's attention. Even if we are simply presenting a short summary at the start of a meeting, our communication skills should be flawless.

To give a good presentation, we need to understand the five questions every audience secretly wants a presenter to answer. If you don't answer these five questions, the audience will tune out. If you do answer them, and you answer them creatively and memorably, the audience will like your presentation.

These questions will look familiar to you because they are the same ancient questions people have been asking of stories since Aristotle first wrote his book *Poetics*.

Nevertheless, when we apply the elements of a good story to a presentation, we get the same result the writers of blockbuster movies get: an engaged and inspired audience.

The five questions are:

1. What problem are you going to help the audience solve?
2. What is your solution to the problem?
3. What will my life look like if I take you up on your solution?

4. What do you want the audience to do next?
5. What do you want the audience to remember?

Many communication coaches will tell you to open with a joke or be vulnerable or breathe deeply before you start talking. All of that advice is fine, but none of that is necessary to give a great presentation. What's necessary for any presentation, whether you're funny or smart or vulnerable or witty, is to answer those five questions for the audience. If you answer those questions, you will win.

For the next four days, I'll introduce you to the Communication Made Simple framework and teach you how to answer those five questions so any audience you stand in front of is impressed with your ability to communicate.

DAY THIRTY-SEVEN
How to Be a Great Communicator—
Give a Great Presentation

Open your talk by telling the audience what problem you are going to help them solve.

It happens to all of us. We step up in front of a group and immediately forget how to start our presentation. We'd rehearsed it a million times, but we didn't realize all those eyes staring at us would make us feel, well, insecure. And so we make the one critical mistake every amateur presenter makes: We fumble into our presentation.

Rather than opening with a strong first line, we make a comment about the weather, or about the coffee, or about how crazy it is that there's a guy in the room you haven't seen since college and you sat near each other in Psychology 101: *Remember Mr. Teamore? Oh my word, he was such a hilarious teacher.*

And the audience checks out because they don't actually care whether you went to college with somebody in the audience and are convinced they wouldn't have found *Mr. Teamore* all that funny.

An audience will not be interested in your presentation until they know you are going to do one thing: Help them solve a problem.

Until you state the problem you are going to help an audience solve, they will wonder:

1. What is this presentation about?
2. Why should we listen to this presentation?
3. Does the speaker even have the authority to be up there?

All good movies start with a problem. And they start with a problem for a reason. The problem is the story hook. Will E.T. get back home? Not sure, let's watch the movie to find out.

Until you state the problem, your audience is wondering why they should pay attention. Start your presentation with a problem.

Are you going to help us stop the annual decline in fourth quarter revenue? Then open the talk by saying, "For the past five years, we've seen a decline in fourth quarter revenue and it's caused most of us to believe this decline is inevitable. I don't believe it is. I think there are three things we can do to see an actual increase in revenue during the fourth quarter."

A statement like this will hook the room and keep them engaged through the entirety of your presentation.

Most presenters don't believe me when I talk about the power of starting with a problem. They take my advice but only partially. They make sure to get to the problem in the first ten minutes or so, but instead of opening with the problem they open with an introduction. They say who they are and where they came from.

Don't.

Instead of opening with an introduction, open with the problem. I speak all the time and I never introduce myself when I first start talking. I introduce myself in the middle of the talk or even at the end. Or, better yet, I just have the announcer introduce me. Why? Because why should I assume anybody cares who I am until they know I can solve an important problem?

When you open your presentation by talking about a problem, you hook the audience. When you don't open with a problem, the audience sits and wonders why they should be listening.

Here's Today's Business Made Simple Tip of the Day

A great communicator starts their presentation by talking about the problem their presentation will help the audience solve.

DAY THIRTY-EIGHT
How to Be a Great Communicator—
Create Subpoints in Your Presentation

A great communicator makes sure all the subpoints in their presentation fit within the boundaries of the overall plot of their talk.

Once you open your talk by stating the problem you will help the audience solve, they will continue to listen to you if you do two things:

1. Reveal a simple plan to help your audience solve their problem.

2. Position each step of the plan as a subplot in the overall narrative.

Stories keep an audience's attention using the devices of plots and subplots, so if you want to keep an audience's attention while giving a talk, your presentation should have plots and subplots too.

When you opened a story loop by clearly defining the problem, you defined the plot of your presentation. The plot of your talk is the controlling idea. Once you define the problem you will help the audience solve, everything else in the presentation needs to fit within the topic of that problem being solved.

That doesn't mean you can't fit a bunch of other ideas into your talk. It's just that you have to find a way for the other topics to fit within the boundaries of your plot.

Years ago, I was asked to write the first draft of the "State of the State" address for a sitting governor. The beginning of the talk was no problem, of course. I simply had the governor state the problem he intended to tackle. The middle of the talk, however, was problematic. It was a long speech and had to cover many different aspects of the state government, including budgetary guidelines. Not the stuff of Hollywood stories.

The speech needed to be both interesting and full of sound bites so the press would cover stories about the governor's agenda.

So, could we keep the audience interested?

The problem we chose to focus on was that there was too much discord between the two major political parties. We wrote about how much better it would be if we come together and how much pain is experienced by citizens if we don't.

This, then, became the controlling idea of the speech. It was all about why we needed to solve the problem of political discord and divisiveness.

From that point on, the speech could go just about anywhere we wanted it to go, even into the minutiae of budgetary spending and overages. I wasn't worried. As long as the controlling idea was that if we come together to help the citizens good things will happen and if we don't the people will experience pain, we could cover any topic and the story would still make sense.

Once we'd chosen the problem, also called "the plot" of the presentation, we needed to get into the plan and the plan needed to have about three (and no more than four) subpoints.

If you intend to cover any more than four subpoints to your major point, your presentation is going to drag. In fact, I recommend no more than three subpoints.

So, what's a subpoint?

Essentially, a subpoint works like a subplot in a story.

A subplot is . . . every story you watch on television or at the movies is made up of plots and subplots.

For instance, a story about a secret agent who needs to get out of a foreign country might be the main plot of the movie but getting from his hotel room to the cab waiting out front without being seen by the spies in the hotel lobby would be a subplot. And then when that subplot closes, the subplot of racing through the streets in a sports car being chased by bad guys on motorcycles opens.

The plot of the story opens a giant story loop by asking a question that is interesting enough that it makes us pay attention for two hours. The subplots of the story, then, are minor questions that get asked and answered during that same two hours that keep an audience interested by moving the action forward.

Here's how a simple story structure looks on paper:

PLOT:	Our hero has to find and arrest a terrorist bomber.
SUBPLOT:	Our hero needs to find the bomb inside the building.
NEXT SUBPLOT:	Our hero finds a riddle next to the bomb that must be solved.
NEXT SUBPLOT:	Our hero realizes the riddle is personal. The bomber knows him.
NEXT SUBPLOT:	Our hero solves the riddle and realizes the bomber is his brother.
NEXT SUBPLOT:	Our hero must find his brother who he hasn't seen in twenty years.

A presentation works just like a Hollywood movie. It's all about plots and subplots.

PLOT:	Democrats and Republicans must come together for the benefit of the people.
SUBPLOT:	We must come together to create education equality.
NEXT SUBPLOT:	We must come together to solve the high cost of medicine.
NEXT SUBPLOT:	We must come together to create tax equality.

By opening and closing subplots within an overarching plot, our presentation will be stitched together with the thread of a single, cohesive story.

If you've ever been bored sitting through a presentation, it's likely because the bullet points in the presentation were not framed as subplots in the overall plot of the presentation itself.

In a screenplay, every scene must advance the hero toward or away from the resolution of a specific problem. If a scene is not framed within the context of the overall plot, it has to go because the audience will get confused and lose interest in the story.

In a good presentation, you will have a single plot with three or four subplots always moving the story forward to a final resolution. This is the way to keep people paying attention all the way through your presentation.

Here's Today's Business Made Simple Tip of the Day

Break your presentation down into plots and subplots, and know your controlling idea before you even get started.

DAY THIRTY-NINE
How to Be a Great Communicator— Foreshadow a Climactic Scene

A great communicator tells the audience what their lives could look like by foreshadowing a climactic scene.

A good story is always headed somewhere, and usually that somewhere has been foreshadowed early enough in the story that the audience knows exactly what they want to happen.

In the movie *Rudy*, we all want Rudy to play in a Notre Dame football game. In *Romeo and Juliet*, we all want Juliet and Romeo to get married. In *The King's Speech*, we all want King George to give a speech without stuttering.

Any good story is headed toward the climactic scene because it's in the climactic scene that all of the tension is resolved, and the audience experiences the joy of a problem resolved.

A great communicator, then, will always foreshadow a climactic scene their audience will experience if they take action on the point the presenter is trying to make.

John F. Kennedy painted the climactic scene of an American astronaut walking on the moon, and America had to vote for him to see that climactic scene happen. "We choose to go to the moon in this decade . . ." Winston Churchill painted a climactic scene that could only happen if Britain bravely fought Hitler: "If we can stand up to him, all Europe may be freed, and the life of the world may move forward into broad and sunlit uplands."

All the world moving *into broad and sunlit uplands,* then, was the foreshadowed climactic scene.

What will life look like if people actually do what your presentation is asking them to do? Have you painted a picture so the audience can imagine that better life? If not, you've not foreshadowed a climactic scene in your talk and your audience has no vision of a better future if they take your advice.

Be sure to make your foreshadowed climactic scene visual. The harder your climactic scene is to visualize, the less power it will have to engage your audience.

When you foreshadow a climactic scene in your presentation, you inspire your audience to head toward that scene. The idea is to make the audience want to make the scene come to life.

Here's Today's Business Made Simple Tip of the Day

Foreshadow a climactic scene in your presentation and you will inspire your audience.

DAY FORTY
How to Be a Great Communicator—Challenge the Audience to Take Action

A great communicator includes a strong call to action in their presentation.

In a good presentation, the audience will be inspired to take action. They will want to "do something" to contribute to an astronaut walking on the moon or see people moving free toward those broad and sunlit uplands.

But what? What can they do? Vote? Fight? Somebody tell me!

A great communicator will include a strong call to action in their presentation so the audience can knowingly contribute to the meaningful effort they recommend.

The main reason you want to include a call to action is because, in general, people do not take action unless they are challenged to take action.

In stories, heroes must be forced to take action by some kind of inciting incident. Their dog has been kidnapped or their husband has been turned into a werewolf!

The strong call to action in your presentation will serve as the inciting incident. It will challenge the audience to do something, and to do something specific.

Another reason to include a strong call to action is because it's only when people take action that they actually believe in an idea.

Call it "skin in the game" if you like, but the idea is when you ask an audience to sacrifice on behalf of an idea or a plan, they begin to own that idea or plan for themselves.

Be careful that your call to action is not elusive. It must be clear.

If you were trying to find a gas station and asked a stranger for directions, them saying *sure, there's a gas station nearby* would not be helpful. Clear directions such as *there's a gas station three blocks up on the right* would get the job done.

To ask an audience to be *more aware* or *care for others* is not a specific enough call to action to be acted upon. Rather, you should ask them to do something like call their representative in Congress and then put that representative's phone number on the screen behind you.

If you are giving a sales presentation, the call to action should be to make an order or schedule a call. If you are giving an internal business presentation, the call to action might be to launch a research team or sell off a division. Regardless, the call to action must be clear.

Around our office, we often repeat a phrase when creating content: Don't make the reader do a bunch of math.

What we mean is, don't make people figure out what you want them to do. Just tell them. And tell them plainly.

Here's Today's Business Made Simple Tip of the Day

Include a strong call to action in your presentation so those hearing it will share ownership of the idea with you.

DAY FORTY-ONE
How to Be a Great Communicator—Determine the Theme of Your Presentation

A great communicator states the theme of their talk at the end of their presentation.

Years ago, I hired a speech coach to help me improve a talk I'd been giving. He came to my office and we spent the better part of two days watching a video of a speech I'd delivered more than a hundred times. Going into the meeting, I thought my speech was pretty terrific. I'd even been getting standing ovations. To my surprise, though, the coach had loads of advice. Turns out I'd only been giving a mediocre speech.

I learned a lot of things, many of which I teach in BMSU's Communication Made Simple course. But the best advice he gave me was to control, with absolute certainty, the last thing I said before walking off the stage.

"People remember the last thing you say more than anything else," he said. "It's like ringing a bell. It just keeps reverberating in their minds for an hour or more."

This was helpful advice to me. The truth is, I'd been leaving the last words of my presentation to chance for a long time. I'd always thank the audience or the host or end the question-and-answer segment by answering the last question, then saying goodnight and walking off the stage.

After learning from my speech coach, I began rehearsing a final line for each speech. I wanted to make sure the thought that rang in their head like a bell for the next hour or more was exactly what I wanted it to be.

This, of course, begs the question: What should your last line be about? What should you say?

The most powerful last line of your presentation should be the theme of your talk.

The idea of a theme also comes from ancient story formulas. Many writers believe all stories stem from a theme. A theme is a way of saying *what the story is about* or *the moral of the story.*

In *Romeo and Juliet*, for example, the theme is *love is worth dying for.* For *The Hunger Games*, it might be *the freedom and dignity of mankind is worth fighting for.*

Like a good story, your presentation can have a theme too. To discover your theme, ask yourself why this presentation is so important. Is it important because all the work that goes into the fourth quarter shouldn't be wasted? Is the theme that *no customer should overpay for lawn care because . . . ?*

In the governor's speech I told you about earlier, the theme was that *citizens shouldn't suffer because Republican and Democratic lawmakers can't get along.*

Stating the theme at the end of your presentation makes sure you told your audience what your talk was about. Without stating the theme, you are making your audience do the math to figure it out for themselves. Chances are, unless you state your theme, they won't be able to figure out the main idea of your talk. And that means you won't be remembered as a good presenter.

How do you determine what the theme of your talk is? Simple. Just fill in the blank in this sentence: *The main point of my presentation is* _____.

Repeat that point several times in your presentation, and of course end the talk by making it the last thing you say, and your audience will leave knowing what you were trying to communicate. Sadly, most audiences have no idea what the presenter was trying to say. They just laughed at a few jokes and sighed at a few emotional stories. And then forgot everything.

When you realize the theme of your presentation, make it your last line. You want your theme to be the idea your audience walks away remembering forever.

In fact, I will often repeat the theme several times throughout my talk, being careful, of course, to state it clearly again at the end of my talk.

Here's Today's Business Made Simple Tip of the Day

End your presentation by stating the theme, so your audience will know why your presentation matters.

A Value-Driven Professional

* *Increase your personal economic value by mastering each core competency.*

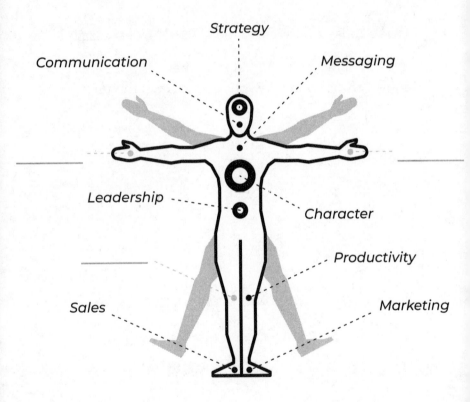

CHAPTER EIGHT

SALES MADE SIMPLE

INTRODUCTION

Having established the character of a competent professional, learned to unite a team around a mission, become more productive, clarified our message, understood what goes into a sales funnel, and become an exceptional communicator, let's talk about how to set up a sales system.

Regardless of whether you run the company or mow the lawn, every professional dramatically increases their value to an organization if they understand how to sell.

Selling is really about clearly explaining to a person how your product or service can solve their problem and then guiding them through a process that leads them to make a purchase.

Most people think selling is about "talking somebody into buying something they don't want," but talking somebody into buying something means you'll likely sell that person one product, one time, and then never sell them anything again.

Human beings resent being coerced into buying things. They may comply, but compliance is often a form of resistance because it's the fastest way to get rid of the salesperson. Plenty of people have driven off the lot in a new car knowing they will never buy from that salesperson again.

A good salesperson, on the other hand, works within a framework that invites a customer into a story in which they solve a problem and feel good about themselves in the process.

A good salesperson makes the customer the hero and helps the hero win the day.

For the next five days, I will give you an overview of the Sales Made Simple framework and it will dramatically increase the number of leads you convert to buyers as well as increase the amount of respect and appreciation you receive from clients.

Once you learn the framework, you'll know which phase of the sales process you are in with each client and be able to offer them the custom help they need. You will also have a sales process that scales. Soon, you'll be excited about engaging new leads because you'll know a significant percentage of them will turn into paying clients.

Making the customer the hero of the story is the key to helping more people and closing more sales.

DAY FORTY-TWO
How to Sell—Qualify the Lead

Cast the right characters: Qualify the lead.

Years ago, I cowrote a movie and the director invited me to help choose the cast. We sat and watched hours of video auditions in which actors would read lines and act out scenes from the script.

Before that experience, I'd have thought the director would simply choose the best actors and move on, but that's not how it works. The truth is, the director chooses the right actor for each part, not necessarily the best actors. Some actors might be more talented, but they are a little too tall or too old or too dramatic or whatever. Really, what a director is looking for in their movie is an actor who fits the role perfectly.

The same is true with sales. When selling, you are inviting a character into a story in which their problem gets solved and they are transformed into a better, more fully equipped version of themselves. This means, however, that not every character is right for the part.

In sales, we call this qualifying the lead. Does the customer have the problem the product solves? Can the customer afford to buy the solution? Does the customer have the authority to buy the product?

It is important for a salesperson to have a list of qualifiers that helps them determine which characters to cast in the story because if you cast the wrong characters, the story won't work.

At my company we have a full-time team member who's only job is to qualify leads. Why? Because going through a sales process with an unqualified lead wastes the customer's time, wastes the sales team's time, and costs you and the company money.

Sales is all about managing your energy and effort. Every minute you spend talking to an unqualified lead would be better spent sleeping under your desk. After all, studies have proven sleep is important to enhance performance, while getting rejected by unqualified leads is crazy making.

So what makes a lead qualified? As mentioned above, a qualified lead meets the following three criteria:

1. They have a problem your product will solve.
2. They are able to afford your product.
3. They have the authority to buy your product.

If your lead is not struggling with the problem you solve, you should move on to another lead. In order to determine this, though, you'll have to fully understand what problem your product actually solves and develop a series of questions to assess whether or not your lead has that problem. Is their insurance plan up for renewal? Are they experiencing hiring difficulties and don't have a team member devoted to HR? Are they out of compliance with a government regulation?

Develop a series of questions that determine whether or not a customer even needs your product or you'll waste valuable energy.

Next, you'll want to find out if the lead can afford your product. Questions like "How much are you currently investing in marketing?" or "What are you currently paying for printing?" are perfectly reasonable to find out if your potential customers' budget restraints will allow them to purchase your product.

If your customer does not have the money to buy your product, politely move on to a more qualified lead.

Lastly, many leads need your product and can even afford your product, but don't have the authority to buy the product. If this is the case, you'll want to develop a relationship with the individual who actually does have the authority.

Ask your lead if they have the authority to make the decision. If they do not, ask them to introduce you to the person who does. Depending on how expensive your product is, even asking your unqualified lead to grab lunch and bring along the qualified lead may be a successful move.

The key here, even before beginning the sales process, is to make sure you are talking to the right person. The right person has a problem your product solves, can afford to buy it, and has the authority to do so.

Every salesperson should keep a long list of qualified leads. Each of these leads is a candidate to be cast in the story you are inviting them into. Consider this list of qualified leads to be the potential cast that will make it into the story. Of course, you haven't actually invited them into the story, but you've done great work weeding out all the candidates who do not fit the role. This phase alone will save you hundreds if not thousands of hours in your effort to solve your customers' problems and change their lives.

Next, let's introduce your lead into the story you want them to live.

> ### Here's Today's Business Made Simple Tip of the Day
>
> Create a list of criteria that qualifies leads so you can move them into a story that solves their problem and changes their lives.

DAY FORTY-THREE
How to Sell—Invite Customers into a Story

Introduce your qualified leads to the story arc your product or service makes possible.

Now that you know who to cast in the story, it's time to invite them into the story itself.

Five things happen in nearly every story. The hero has a problem, that problem is frustrating them so much they want to take action, they meet a guide who has some kind of plan or tool to help them, they begin to believe in the solution, and then they take action to resolve their problem.

So, in order for your qualified leads to get interested in stepping into that story, you simply need to lay the story out for them.

To create a custom story arc for every one of your clients, you will want to use this formula:

1. I see you are struggling with X problem.
2. I see that X problem is causing Y frustration.
3. Our product or service resolves Y frustration by resolving X problem.
4. We've worked with hundreds of clients with X problems and here are their results.
5. Let's create a step-by-step plan so your problem and frustration get resolved.

This formula has been used for thousands of years to tell stories because the human mind understands it and is drawn to it. So, if the human mind understands this formula and is drawn to it, you should use this formula to invite customers into a story in which their problems are resolved through the purchasing of your products.

As you better understand the framework, you will learn to be disciplined in the story you invite customers into. Too many salespeople veer off into the weeds when it comes to selling and that's why they don't close very many sales.

Instead of sending gifts and thank-you cards and calling your clients on their birthdays, do the hard work of identifying their problems, listening to the frustrations that their problems are causing, and consulting with them over how those problems can be solved.

The goal of a good salesperson should not be to be liked; it should be to be trusted. We like just about anybody who is nice to us, but we trust and respect people who can ease our frustrations by helping us solve problems.

When you talk with a potential customer, do you clearly see and can you clearly explain the story you are inviting them into? And can you customize that story for their specific situation and pain points? And are you communicating that story as an invitation to solve their problems and change their lives?

If not, use the five-part formula above to map your customers' stories and then start inviting them to resolve their problem. If you do, you will find that the respect and trust you receive, along with the sales you close, will increase.

> **Here's Today's Business Made Simple Tip of the Day**
>
> Identify your customers' problems and invite them into a story in which their problems are resolved.

DAY FORTY-FOUR
How to Sell—Repeat Your Talking Points

Play the guide and know your lines.

Most potential customers do not walk away from a purchase because the salesperson failed to be charming, friendly, or challenging. They walk away from a purchase because the salesperson failed to guide them toward a resolution to their problem.

How can we get more sales? We can play the guide.

By now, you know the roles that exist in every story. You also know that, as far as selling goes, the customer is the hero.

The story is all about them. That said, we do play an important role in the story. We play the guide.

Obi-Wan Kenobi was a guide to Luke Skywalker in *Star Wars*. Haymitch was a guide to Katniss in *The Hunger Games*. You are a guide for your customer.

So, what does a guide do? Well, as it relates to selling, a guide does three things:

1. Reminds the hero what the story is about.
2. Gives the hero a plan to resolve their problem and win the day.
3. Foreshadows the climactic scene of the story.

In order to play the guide, we need to continually remind our customers what the story is about and invite them to step into that story so they can experience a positive resolution.

A guide needs to know their lines and speak them often. Reminding the customer about the story and offering them a plan comes down to talking points.

If I'm selling children's playground equipment and my customer is a local church, my lines are:

> I know you're looking for a way for your church to be more inviting to the community and it's frustrating to try to relay how welcoming you really are. After you install the playground and invite the community to the grand opening, you will have sent a warm message and more folks will feel a connection with the congregation. I think that will result in more people in church and more lives being changed.

Did you catch the story, the plan, and the climactic scene?

The problem: The community doesn't come to church because they don't perceive the church building as inviting.

The plan: Build a playground and invite the community to the grand opening.

The climactic scene: ". . . more people in church and more lives being changed."

These lines, or variations thereof, become the guide's talking points.

Memorize Your Talking Points

The key to inviting customers into a story is to figure out the talking points that define the story and then repeat them in lunch meetings, emails, proposals, phone calls, and more.

Many salespeople spend ages trying to build rapport. That's nice. But our job as salespeople is to solve problems and change lives. And, honestly, nothing builds rapport faster than solving problems and changing lives.

To be sure, repeating lines to a customer without having meaningful conversations may come off as off-putting. But the nice thing about having prepared talking points for each of your potential customers is it allows you to spend the majority of your time together talking about other things. So 80 percent of your time can be spent building an authentic relationship as long as 20 percent of your communication is reinforcing the talking points and inviting the customer into a clear and compelling story.

When you're together with a customer, it's a good thing to open and close with your talking points as a way of making sure your customer understands the story you are inviting them into.

Just like a leader going into an important speech or interview, a good salesperson has their talking points memorized and repeats them over and over. If they do, the customer will recognize the salesperson as a guide in their life, find themselves invited into a compelling story, and make a purchase that solves their problem.

Always remember, the customer is the hero. And they're looking for a guide to invite them into a story. This is what being a salesperson is all about.

> ### Here's Today's Business Made Simple Tip of the Day
>
> Prepare defined talking points that invite customers into a story and repeat those talking points over and over.

DAY FORTY-FIVE
How to Sell—Create a Great Proposal

Lay out your proposal using the formula of a storybook.

Many salespeople will summarize their offer in bullet points within a hastily sent email and then be surprised when their customer rejects the offer.

Often, the customer will blame their decision not to buy on price, competition, schedule, budgetary concerns, and so on. But I doubt any of those excuses are completely accurate.

The reality is, the customer was most likely confused about how the transaction was going to work and what they would be getting out of the deal. People always reject a confusing offer.

For this reason, memorialize the story points of the offer inside a proposal, brochure, or even a video.

In sales pitches, as we get to know our customers' problems, lay out a plan, and foreshadow a climactic scene for their lives, we should not assume they will remember every word, or that they have taken notes and spent hours studying our proposal. It's more likely they enjoyed the conversations, were enticed by the narrative invitation, and then went home and forgot the details.

Then, when it came time to make a decision, they felt confused.

Whenever a customer tells you they will think about it and get back to you later, you likely believe that means they are rejecting your offer. Actually, I don't think they are rejecting your offer at all. What they are really saying is, "I'll get back to you when I have more clarity." Sadly, the clarity never comes. Why? Because you never gave it to them in a single, interesting document they could read and review.

This is why a good proposal, brochure, website, video, or any other piece of collateral we create to close the sale is so important.

People do not like to walk into a fog. Our internal survival mechanisms want us to stay in environments that are free of threats or potential threats, and walking into a fog involves too much mystery.

The same is true in the world of ideas. If we are confused about what the future looks like, about what somebody's intentions are, or even about what our next steps should be, the brain senses mental fog and steps back.

Great salespeople create a proposal template and then customize each proposal for the client. They thoughtfully relay the customer's problems, the specific plan they discussed, and the strong call to action that leads to the climactic scene.

Here is a template for a good proposal:

1. The customer's problem
2. The product that will solve the problem

3. The plan to implement the solution (product) into the customer's life
4. The price and options
5. The climactic scene (the result of the resolution of the problem)

This is a simple story formula not unlike one you'd find in a children's book. It is easy to understand, and the premise within it (that the product can solve the customer's problem) is easy to understand based on how it's been presented.

A proposal, PDF, or video that lays out the customer's story in this form is easy to understand, creates no fog or confusion, and is more likely to result in a sale.

Proposals may seem out of date, slow, and unnecessary, but the truth is, they are a great service to our customers and they close deals.

A good salesperson will spend their downtime looking over their database, recalling their customers' problems and needs for a solution, and then customizing proposals to send for their review. This salesperson will close more sales than any other. Why? Because they took the time to memorialize the customer's story and create clarity around the decision they want the customer to make.

Here's Today's Business Made Simple Tip of the Day

Use a proposal or some other piece of sales collateral to memorialize the customer's story so the customer has a document that alleviates confusion and helps them make a decision.

DAY FORTY-SIX
How to Sell—How to Close the Sale

A great sales professional calls customers to action with confidence.

I knew a guy in high school who dated all the pretty girls. Always the gentleman, he'd go up and talk to them and make them laugh, and if they struck his interest, he'd ask them out. He didn't have any fear at all and the girls appreciated it. They liked that he made things light and fun and didn't pressure them. He didn't seem to care if they rejected him, either. He'd just keep it light so they didn't feel bad about making him feel bad. And they liked him even more for that.

Me and my friends, however, would make too big a deal out of those early relationships. We believed that if we asked a girl out and she said no, she'd never talk to us again or would tell her friends we were creeps. Instead, we'd try to feel out the situation and ask confusing questions like what kind of shampoo does she use and does she tie her own bow and all sorts of other questions that are the worst things you could possibly say if you ever want to date.

Once, when we asked my friend how he got so bold in talking to girls, he smiled and said, *Man, just don't make it heavy.*

That wasn't just good advice about dating. That was good advice about life.

It took years for me to realize that dating was just dating, and that rejection was part of life and nobody should feel bad about it.

I believe the same is true in sales. The reason people get nervous about dating is the same reason some salespeople are afraid to close the deal. They're nervous about being rejected. They're making it heavy.

The truth is, if you aren't a creep and treat people with the utmost respect and believe you can benefit the lives around you, there should be nothing heavy about a sales interaction.

Sales is part of life and nobody should feel awkward about it. Sales professionals do better when we fully live as salespeople, telling everybody what we sell and what problems our products solve and asking people to tell their friends about our products.

If we're going to be good salespeople, we have to get over the fear of rejection.

The most important part of the sales process is the call to action. Every salesperson knows that. But it's the sales professional who feels terrific about their call to action, understands it as a service to the world, and does not make it heavy who actually gets the sale.

When I'm talking with a potential customer (or, for that matter, a friend, family member, or bus driver), I'll often be heard saying, "Your people need you to help them develop themselves because they can't afford to go back to college. You should get them signed up for my online learning platform, Business Made Simple. They'll become great business professionals and feel cared about by you."

Why do I let people know about my product so often? Because I spent years floundering around in college and never learned what I needed to learn to be of value inside an organization. After learning what I needed to know from books and friends and failures and becoming a successful business owner myself, I wanted to make the process easier for others. I believe in my product. I believe I can solve a serious problem in the world and so I'm not shy about letting people know.

In short, I believe I can invite people into a story that will transform their lives. Why should I be shy about that?

Do you believe in the product you sell? Do you believe you can solve a customer's problem and change their life? If you don't, quit. I'm serious. Just walk away from the company and find a mission you believe in.

I could teach you a sales process all day, but if you don't believe in yourself or your product, it won't work.

Most of the problems salespeople have in closing deals are psychological. Their problems stem from thinking of rejection as heavy and so they make sales conversations awkward. Their problems come from not believing in themselves. Their problems come from not believing in their products.

When we believe in ourselves and our products, we do not act in fear—rather, we call customers to action with confidence.

Here's Today's Business Made Simple Tip of the Day

Do not fear rejection, but call your customers to action with confidence.

A Value-Driven Professional

* *Increase your personal economic value by mastering each core competency.*

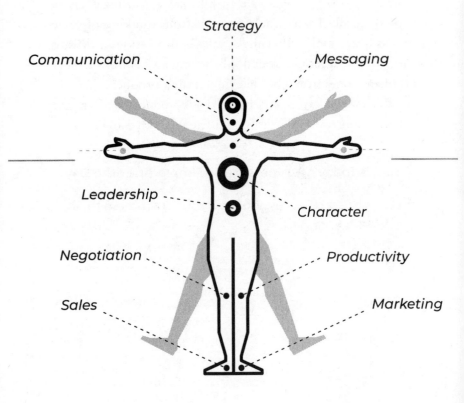

CHAPTER NINE

NEGOTIATION MADE SIMPLE

INTRODUCTION

Having established the character of a competent professional, learned to unite a team around a mission, become more productive, clarified our message, understood what goes into a sales funnel, become an exceptional communicator, and learned to sell, let's learn how to be a terrific negotiator.

Every professional is constantly negotiating, whether they know it or not. They negotiate their salary with their boss, their schedule with their assistant, a contract with a supplier, and even what restaurant they and their friends will eat at for lunch.

Anytime you find yourself in strategic communication in order to win a deal or resolve a problem, you are in a negotiation.

A good negotiator can make or save a company millions each year. Therefore, any team member who understands a negotiation framework dramatically increases their value inside an organization.

Sadly, most professionals negotiate without ever realizing they are negotiating at all. When they find themselves in conversations that involve making a decision, they think they are just having a conversation. And because of this, most professionals don't get what they want for themselves or for the company they work for.

Less than 10 percent of working professionals have been trained in a negotiation course. This presents a strategic opportunity for the rest of us to increase our personal economic value.

John Lowry, who teaches Business Made Simple's Negotiation Made Simple course, says that if you don't have a strategic negotiation framework to use, you're probably going to lose.

He's right.

When negotiating, don't trust your gut. Trust a proven process.

In the next four days, I'll introduce you to four of the many points John makes in the negotiation course he teaches for Business Made Simple and at Pepperdine Law.

I've taken John's class three times. Each time I take the class, I learn something new. In fact, his class taught me several significant moves I've made in negotiating contracts that have netted me millions.

I've compiled my four favorite takeaways from John's course because these are the four takeaways that have made or saved me money directly. If you understand these four principles, you are going to be a better negotiator than nearly anybody else you know. And a good negotiator is a valued member of any team.

DAY FORTY-SEVEN
How to Negotiate—the Two Types of Negotiations

A good negotiator understands the two different kinds of negotiations, collaborative and competitive.

Not everybody sees a negotiation the same way at the same time. Some modes of negotiation play out like a win/lose game, while others play out like an attempt to find a win/win solution.

Within a long-term negotiation, in fact, the mode of negotiation can change from win/win to win/lose, and if you don't know the switch has been made, you will certainly suffer in the negotiation.

A win/lose mode of negotiation is called competitive while a win/win mode is called collaborative.

A general rule about negotiation is that if one party is competitive and the other party is collaborative, the competitive negotiation technique is going to win and the collaborative will lose. Nearly always.

But this doesn't mean competitive negotiators always win. If two negotiators enter into a negotiation, one of them will certainly lose while the other wins.

When in a competitive mode, negotiators don't just need to be pleased with the result; they need you to be displeased. Again, when in a competitive mode, the negotiator will not sense that they have won until you have lost.

When in a collaborative negotiation mode, however, the negotiator is looking for both parties to benefit from the deal.

So here's the rule: If you are in a collaborative negotiation mode and you sense the person you are negotiating with is in a competitive mode, you should switch to competitive immediately. Why? Because they are not looking for a win/win, and in order to create a win/win scenario, you need for them to join you.

So how does this play out? Well, recently I negotiated the purchase of a commercial property. My default negotiation mode is collaborative so I'm always looking for a win/win scenario. It became clear the team I was negotiating with wasn't interested in understanding what I wanted, only in getting what they wanted, so I quickly switched my mode to competitive. We went back and forth on price until the price finally came to the number I wanted. But rather than shaking hands and saying "we both win," I let them know this was a lot of money and I would have to make a significant sacrifice to make it happen. I let them know I'd love for the price to be lower and asked again if they could come down. They refused. So I did the deal.

Why was it important for me not to let them know we'd arrived at the price I wanted? Because if they knew we both won, they'd raise the price. A competitive negotiator needs for you to lose, so when you let them know all you are losing to do the deal, they are satisfied.

Is this deceptive? That's not how I see it. The truth is, I did have to sacrifice to do the deal and I'd love to have purchased the building for less, and if they wanted me to be upset about the deal, why not give them what they want? After all, that's the only way to get the deal done. Remember, when in competitive mode, a negotiator will not stop until they are sure you have lost.

What we're really talking about here is creating a false bottom to the negotiation. When in competitive mode, the competitive negotiator will continue to drive the price down until you can't go any further. When you realize the negotiation has gone competitive, then, make sure to let them know you won't be able to go any further and that's when they will feel as though they have won.

Here's the warning: Don't be naive. When in competitive mode, a negotiator wants you to lose. When in collaborative mode, a negotiator wants both parties to win. Neither mode is better than the other. They both work great. But if you are in collaborative mode and the other party is competitive, you will lose unless you recognize what is happening.

Always know what kind of negotiation mode the person you are negotiating with is in and respond accordingly.

Here's Today's Business Made Simple Tip of the Day

Always know whether you are in a competitive or collaborative negotiation, and negotiate accordingly.

DAY FORTY-EIGHT
How to Negotiate—Go Below the Line

A good negotiator goes below the line.

Not all negotiations are rational. Human beings are complex, and often emotional issues come into play during a negotiation. People are motivated by many things, not just money.

As I was building my company, I had to find a way to attract rock star talent that would normally only want to work at a larger company. I began listing "other benefits" that came with working on our team. The first was we were clearly on a meaningful mission, and that was attractive to them. Another reason was because, for each position, we could offer something more valuable than pay. We could offer them a small platform where they could grow their personal influence or the chance to work from home or the ability to work with a team of high-performing individuals. One of the ways we built such a terrific team early on was to highlight the extra opportunities people would get if they joined our team.

John Lowry, the teacher who teaches Business Made Simple's Negotiation Made Simple course, calls this going below the line.

As you negotiate, ask yourself what other factors could be in play. Does the seller want the car to go to somebody who will love it and take care of it the way she did? If you're the buyer who will take good care of that car, make sure to spell out how you're going to continue the tradition. Would the buyer be willing to pay more if they knew this was the same jar of peanut butter Elvis ate from just before he died? If you're talking to a crazy Elvis fan, that would be an important "below the line" fact to bring up!

Once, while negotiating a large business deal, I was able to create a win/win scenario by getting a well-known speaker to speak at one of my events by agreeing to help them craft their talk in such a way that it could later be turned into a book. Did the speaker come because I paid them so much? No, they came because I was able to help them think through their material and future manuscript.

John Lowry is right. There is almost always something happening below the line. A good negotiator is going to understand that a negotiation is about more than just numbers; it's about bringing somebody satisfaction at the end of the deal. And that includes emotional satisfaction.

Do you make a habit of looking for what's below the line in your negotiations?

Here's Today's Business Made Simple Tip of the Day

When negotiating a deal, find out if there is anything below the line you can offer your counterpart as a way of making the deal more satisfying and bringing it to a close.

DAY FORTY-NINE
How to Negotiate—Make the Initial Offer

A good negotiator anchors the negotiation with the initial offer.

Negotiation scholars often disagree about whether or not you should make the opening offer. The logic for not making the opening offer goes like this: If you wait for the other side to speak first, you'll learn what they want and find clues about what it will take to close the deal.

That makes sense because you often won't know the range the other side is considering. And yet by letting the other side make the opening offer, you lose something I think is more valuable. You lose the ability to anchor the negotiation.

Anchoring the negotiation means that you've placed a number on the table that you want the rest of the negation to gravitate around.

For instance, if you're buying a new car, the dealership puts a number on the window that almost always anchors the price with a high gravitational pull. If they want $35,000 for the car, and you negotiate the price down to $34,000, you feel like you got a deal at $1,000 off the asking price. But what if the opening offer (the sticker on the car) was set $5,000 over

164 BUSINESS MADE SIMPLE

what the dealership was willing to accept? That means they actually got $4,000 over the price they'd have sold it for.

When you are able to make the opening offer, you, from that point on, set the gravitational anchor for the rest of the conversation. This is a strategic advantage.

Let's say, though, you weren't able to set the opening offer. Real estate and automobiles, for example, have the opening offer set before you even start negotiating. If this is the case, you can adjust the gravity of the negotiation a bit more your way by setting the gravitational pull with a counteroffer. A counteroffer isn't as strong as the opening offer, but it's still helpful.

Sometimes, having information that adjusts the gravity of the negotiation your way resets the conversation. A friend who worked in the car business recently sat down at a luxury car dealership to buy a new car. My friend sold the software that many car dealerships use to track their inventory. The salesman stated the price at $90,000. My friend then pulled out a printout of a report on the car stating how the dealership had bought the car for $60,000 and he felt $70,000 would be a fair price, allowing the dealership to make a $10,000 profit. That bit of information reset the gravity of the negotiation in my friend's favor. He was able to buy the $90,000 car for $72,000.

Regardless of whether you make the opening offer or not, by thinking of various offers as numbers that affect the gravitational pull, you can sway the deal more toward a resolution you are comfortable with.

> ### Here's Today's Business Made Simple Tip of the Day
>
> Make the opening offer and establish an anchor for the rest of the negotiation.

DAY FIFTY
How to Negotiate—Don't Get Emotionally Hooked

A good negotiator diversifies their interests to avoid being emotionally hooked.

As I mentioned in an earlier entry, we aren't exactly rational human beings when it comes to negotiation. For this reason, when we are negotiating for something we want, we should make sure we aren't overtaken by our emotions so that we make a bad decision.

We've all been in negotiations where we find ourselves wanting whatever it is we are negotiating for a little too much. Whether it's a house, a car, a new team member, or even a relationship, the power in the negotiation suddenly shifts toward the other side. We want whatever it is and we will sacrifice whatever it takes.

This is a bad place to be in a negotiation.

But what do we do when we are overcome with emotion?

One good tactic is to find another alternative and split our interests so that we aren't so easily carried away.

For instance, years ago my wife and I began negotiating to buy our neighbor's house. Our plan was to buy his house, tear it down and build a new house, and use our current home as a guest house. We entertain more than two hundred overnight guests each year and so we needed the space.

The truth is, the price our neighbor was asking was too high. He was basing his evaluation on comparable properties that were in a much more sought-after part of town. Still, I found myself walking around the backyard imagining our dream home right there where my neighbor's house stood. It was all I could do not to just go offer him the money.

Instead, though, I remembered what John Lowry taught me in his course. When you are emotionally hooked, split your interest and begin to look for alternatives.

When we feel like whatever it is we are negotiating for is the only one of its kind, we enter into a scarcity mindset and lose emotional leverage.

Instead of making an offer to my neighbor, I called my real estate agent and asked him to make a low offer on fifteen acres down the street. I'd found the property years before but it was way over our budget and so I never inquired about it.

My real estate agent reluctantly made an offer on the other piece of property (I say reluctantly because the offer was so low my agent thought it might even be insulting) and, to all our surprise, the buyer wanted to talk. A few months later, my wife and I closed on the fifteen acres at two-thirds the asking price. We couldn't believe it.

It's funny how you can want something so badly when you think there's nothing better out there, but the second you split your interest, you gain leveraging power and also realize a scarcity mindset could cost you.

The strategy here is to beware of wanting something so much. Wanting something too much hooks you, and once you're hooked, you'll likely start making bad decisions. There is a world of wonderful options out there. Make sure you know what they are before you start negotiating.

Here's Today's Business Made Simple Tip of the Day

Diversify your interest in an opportunity before you start negotiating to avoid being emotionally hooked.

A Value-Driven Professional

* *Increase your personal economic value by mastering each core competency.*

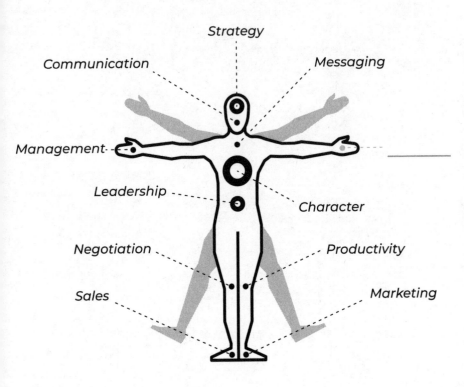

CHAPTER TEN

MANAGEMENT MADE SIMPLE

INTRODUCTION

So far in this book, we've covered eight characteristics of a value-driven professional: how to unite a team around a mission, personal productivity, how a business really works, messaging, marketing, communication, sales, and negotiation. We are without question a much more valuable professional than we were when we started. But let's add even more value by talking about something most of us have to do every day: manage people.

Management is all about helping other people win so the overall team can win. Managers who are not liked are managers who do not have a clear definition of what it means to win or don't have a clear idea of the wins each individual team member can experience personally while they are helping the overall team win.

In short, we trust professional leaders for two reasons:

1. They know what they are doing and can help the team win.

2. They care about each individual on the team.

A good manager is able to analyze the skills and talent on their team and design a winning plan around that team.

In the next section of the book, I'm going to talk about creating and running an execution program. The truth is, though, I see management and execution as two sides of the same coin. Management, however, is about creatively putting the right people to work on the right assignments. Management creates systems, and execution manages those systems.

A good manager will both dream up a system or process and then manage its execution straight through until the results are excellent.

Managers are everywhere, even if they aren't called managers. Every team member that is given the freedom to improve upon their job is actually a manager. They are a manager because they must identify what is important and create processes that get the important things done better and faster.

Even if you work by yourself in your own company, you are a manager. You must do your work smarter, faster, and better so that you create tangible value and have the highest chance of success.

Of course, we must always remember that when we manage we aren't just managing systems, we are managing people within those systems.

In the next five days, I'll introduce you to the Management Made Simple framework that will help anybody from a first-time manager to a seasoned professional improve their management skills.

The Management Made Simple framework is a unique take on management, reaching beyond the soft skills of people management and into the arena of what it takes to build a high-performing team.

The objective behind the Management Made Simple framework is to give every team member a manager they love, and every profit and loss statement a bottom line that signals victory.

DAY FIFTY-ONE
How to Manage People—Establish Clear Priorities

A great manager establishes clear priorities.

The number one job of a manager is to have a crystal clear understanding about their division's priorities. To do this, I make sure every manager of every division of my company knows what they are responsible to produce. Whether it's closed sales contracts, leads, finished pieces of curriculum, or subscription renewals, each division of every company exists to add something to the bottom line. Each division's priorities should be a building block for whatever it is that division is responsible to make. By deciding what your priorities are, you are defining for yourself and every member of your team a focus.

This sounds simple and trivial, but half the managers I talk to do not know what their department is supposed to produce. And even if they are certain, when I talk to individual members of their team, I get different answers.

Nobody can read their manager's mind. The manager must tell the team, nearly every day, what their focus should be.

Another mistake managers make in defining what their division produces is that they are vague. If they run a customer service team, the manager may say something like, "We produce customer satisfaction," which sounds nice, but is difficult to measure and even more difficult to know how to directly produce.

Producing smiles and happy people is terrific marketing copy, but a good manager is more practical.

For instance, a manager of a customer service division should aim to produce something tangible, like 100 percent completed customer service tickets within thirty minutes of receiving them. If knowing that having their requests responded to in thirty minutes or less dramatically increases customer satisfaction, the team then knows how to produce the whole through the sum of its parts.

I know this sounds like semantics, but the semantics are important. As managers, we must clearly define what it is our division (or company) produces.

When deciding what your division (or your company) produces, it is important that whatever you choose has three characteristics:

1. It must be measurable.
2. It must be profitable.
3. It must be scalable.

It Must Be Measurable

Do you know what you produce and can you measure it?

If we are running a restaurant, we want to measure something like the time we cook the food and the amount of time it takes to get that food to a table because, if we do not, we are likely to have cold food being delivered to tables, which will result in unhappy, dissatisfied diners.

If I were interviewing a potential manager and they told me their first step would be to break down the parts of the process that produce something for the company's bottom line, then begin to measure those parts to keep the team accountable to accomplish them, they would stand out as a manager who knows what they are doing. Again, most managers think their job is to manage people and they give no thought to a process, but people thrive when they are given clear processes and priorities.

It Must Be Profitable

Whatever each department produces, it must be directly associated with the bottom line of the organization.

It is not enough that my events department produces events. They must produce profitable events. If my events director thinks their job is to simply produce events, they may produce fifty events that are unprofitable and sink the company.

This is important because there are many managers who will do exactly that. They will see their job as a series of tasks that had been dictated to them by their boss and feel they must simply execute those tasks. This is not a manager. This is a low-level worker. Managers must always be aware of how their production affects revenue and profit.

If a manager works for a boss who does not think about revenue and profit, yet the manager does, that manger will take their boss's job in short order.

The bottom line of a company is the bottom line. If the company is not profitable, the company will go under and everybody will lose their jobs. CEOs and company presidents know this and feel a kindred spirit with managers who understand the pressure of this dynamic.

It Must Be Scalable

Lastly, whatever it is you produce must be scalable. This is not true for businesses that don't desire to scale, but for most of us, it's critical. If a manager creates processes to create product and those processes do not profitably scale, the organization is capped.

Could more people be hired to create more of whatever it is that you're obligated to produce? Is the process you've designed dependent on you or other employees' personalities or skill sets to deliver en masse? Have you so clearly defined the processes that must be performed that somebody else could join the team and accomplish those processes to increase production?

A value-driven professional knows how to manage a division by determining something specific their division produces. The criteria for whatever it is they decide to produce, then, must be measurable, profitable, and scalable.

It is my view that knowing what to produce and making sure it is measurable, profitable, and scalable is a significant percentage of a manager's job.

Sadly, very few managers even know this is part of their job. Most first-time managers establish weekly meetings with their direct reports and simply ask the question "how are we doing?" While this may seem like a thoughtful question, it is anything but helpful. This manager's direct report has no idea what they are supposed to produce and what they are supposed to focus on, and has no way to measure their performance.

A manager who just wants to check in with people is more interested in being liked than being respected and trusted. While that is great for the manager's sense of well-being, it's terrible for their team members and the bottom line of the organization.

Human beings want to be part of a big story, a story about building something worthwhile. And human beings like to measure their progress and see, at the end of a year, that the thing they built is bigger than it was when they started.

A manager should want something more than to be liked. They should want to create a team in which every member feels valuable and important based on a performance that is measurable.

Let's be both liked and respected by clearly defining what it is our division is supposed to produce and then keeping our team accountable to accomplish repeatable, specific tasks that affect that production.

A good manager asks "how can we do better?" based on the numbers both the manager and direct report are responsible for producing.

Defining what each division produces leads to a clarity of purpose and expectations. Clarity leads to trust and respect for the manager who defined those expectations.

Here's Today's Business Made Simple Tip of the Day

A good manager knows how to define a specific output that is measurable, profitable, and scalable.

DAY FIFTY-TWO
How to Manage People—Identify Key Performance Indicators

Identify the key performance indicators you will measure.

The second thing a good manager does is identify and measure key performance indicators.

A good manager loves to measure things. They love numbers as much as they love people because numbers tell them how to challenge their team, how to grow their team, and when to celebrate their team's various victories. The team that works for you is always wondering how they are doing, and unless you are able to measure progress around key performance indicators, you won't be able to tell them.

Once we define what our department produces, we must measure the factors that lead to the production of that output.

By deciding what to measure, we tell ourselves and the members of our teams what specific routine tasks are important. In the end, knowing what specific, repeatable tasks a team member is responsible for adds to clarity—and remember, clarity from a manager leads to trust and respect.

Once you define what it is your department produces, you'll want to figure out the lead indicators that are causing that production. Lead indicators are the actions that lead to success while lag indicators are the measurements of that success.

For instance, one thousand sales in the month of January is a lag indicator. Those sales have already happened and there's nothing we can do to increase them. The month is done.

Making sure each of our sales representatives makes fifteen calls per day, however, is a lead indicator that causes the lag indicator. That's why good managers are actually as obsessed with lead indicators as they are with lag indicators: because lead indicators cause lag indicators.

If I had just been given the job of sales director, my first priority would be to figure out what causes sales to happen. Likely, those indicators would be calls made, which by necessity means leads attained. I'd also likely find that when we trigger an automated email campaign as a response to a primary sales call, sales go up. And then they go up even further when we send a formal proposal. So, what will I want to measure? Leads, initial calls, email campaign launches, and formal proposals sent.

I may also find that when it comes to our top-tier deals, the CEO calling to back up the proposal closes 70 percent more business. So, with the CEO's approval, I'm going to add that as a lead indicator too.

A good manager knows how to see the process for its parts and measure the production of each part in the assembly of the whole.

Measuring positive indicators, though, is not the only priority. A good manager will also manage potential problems. They will want to know when it is most likely that their assembly line will break down and measure hours used on various machines to trigger maintenance calls that prevent stoppage.

If we do not measure the specific indicators that increase production, we leave the focus of our people and our division up to chance. And chance rarely produces anything good.

A good manager acts like a coach. They explain the rules of the game to their team and give them specific instructions about how to perform better and win the game.

A manager who simply cheers their team on is not a coach; they are a cheerleader. Coaches design plays, give specific instructions, and collaborate with their team to create strategies that lead to victory.

To determine what to classify as a key performance indicator, you'll want to reverse engineer the components of the products you are supposed to produce.

If a specific division's job is to produce social media collateral that sells product, for example, the key performance indicators might be:

1. Five specific and helpful Instagram, Facebook, and Twitter posts highlighting benefits of the product
2. Three customer testimonials about the transformational power of the product
3. Two direct offers per month including an expiring bonus

These specific components, of course, lead to orders. If these key performance indicators are met week after week, the bottom line of the company will be positively affected.

One last note. Each lead indicator should be compared to a standard. A standard number will help you know whether you have met or failed to meet your daily, weekly, or monthly goal. If we were supposed to make a hundred sales calls this week but only completed seventy-five, we should analyze the machine to see what needs to be adjusted. Perhaps our expectations were too high? Or, perhaps, our performance was too low? These are the questions a good manager obsesses over.

Figuring out your key performance indicators is really about fully understanding how a machine works in order to measure its efficiency and output.

Without measurements, you will be guessing. If you guess, somebody will come along who actually knows what to measure and they will take your job.

Don't let that happen.

Figure out what to measure and become obsessed with increasing the quantity and quality of whatever it is that you or your division produces.

Some people will see this idea of management as akin to turning human beings into cogs in a machine. But this is hardly the case. What we are really doing is creating a game and a scoreboard so that everybody can understand the rules and enjoy the game.

A good manager knows how to create a game out of their work and further knows how to guide their team members to victory.

Here's Today's Business Made Simple Tip of the Day

Determine what key performance indicators lead to the successful output of your end product and then measure those indicators.

DAY FIFTY-THREE
How to Manage People—Create Streamlined Processes

Create processes that increase the activity-to-output ratio.

Now that we know what we are supposed to produce and are measuring lead indicators that cause that production, it's time to increase the efficiency of the machine we are responsible for managing.

The difference between a value-driven professional and an average team member is that the value-driven professional is going to think creatively about improving the performance of the machine.

A value-driven professional can create the machine, measure its output, and then tune the engine for higher and higher efficiency and productivity.

But how do you make the machine that is your department more efficient? Simply ask the question: *How could we make this better?*

Most of the professionals you work with are smart and talented, so don't improve your processes in a vacuum. Hold a series of meetings in which you and your team analyze your processes and answer the question: *How can we make things better?* It will likely be your team, not you, who have the insight. In addition, when you include your team, you will get more buy-in for the improved way you will be doing things.

Making the machine more efficient is the hallmark of a great manager. Roy Kroc, upon buying McDonald's, drew out his restaurants in chalk, making sure each team member knew specific tasks while operating in a specific station to sell more hamburgers.

While most of us don't run fast-food restaurants, we all would make more money if we analyzed our processes and created systems that increase the activity-to-output ratio. Much money is lost in inefficiencies, and managers who know this and fix this are given more responsibility.

Again, making the machine more efficient is about improving the activity-to-output ratio. We want to constantly ask ourselves how we can get more output out of our activity. The answer to this question might involve moving the equipment around in your shop so that people and parts don't have to travel so far. It might mean jobbing out certain tasks or cutting a weak revenue stream to save bandwidth for more profitable activity.

The underlying question is: *How can we produce more of what we produce without losing quality or increasing activity?*

Another question you want to ask in order to improve the output and efficiency of your division is: *What is the limiting factor in our division, and how can we decrease that limitation?*

Are you spending too much time on the phone with unqualified clients? Is there a machine that everybody has to wait for and it makes sense to buy a second machine? Is a specific team member not performing to a certain standard? What is causing inefficiency in the machine you are responsible for running?

A good manager will ask these questions every day and then make the changes necessary to increase the activity-to-output ratio.

Here's Today's Business Made Simple Tip of the Day

Improve the output and efficiency of yourself and your division by asking what limiting factors are holding you back.

DAY FIFTY-FOUR
How to Manage People—Give Valuable Feedback

Give valuable feedback early and often.

The processes we are creating and improving upon are built and sustained by giving valuable feedback. Once, while attending a Seattle Seahawks practice with my COO, I remarked at how efficiently the team went through their drills. They literally ran through every play they'd run for the coming game in only forty-five minutes. The team members entered and exited the field responding to a few whistles. Everything about the practice had been turned into processes that had been memorized, and like a Swiss watch they were run with precision.

What really made the practice work, though, was what happened at the end. Coach Carroll brought the team close and celebrated the wins from that practice. Why? Because you will never turn a human being into a machine. They must always receive human connection and human affirmation.

People are infinitely more complex and miraculous than machines. Machines cannot assess beauty, value, or meaning from a nuanced world. Machines cannot empathize with you or actually care about your well-being in a way that is emotionally relevant or comforting.

A good manager knows, then, that their people are their most valuable asset, and while they work to create a better and better machine, they treat the people who build that machine with great care.

The proper care of people, in a professional setting, involves letting them know how they are doing as members of the team. And this involves praise and constructive feedback.

When giving praise, be specific about what the team member has done to earn that praise. When we say "good job," we shouldn't assume the team member knows which aspect of the job they should actually repeat. Comments like "Way to stay calm under pressure" or "Good job putting in the extra time to get that right" are more specific.

Praising our team members is easy. Sadly, praise is only half the job of managing people. Offering constructive feedback is the other half.

Many first-time managers fear giving constructive feedback at all. They don't mind praising their team members, but conversations that involve criticism feel heavy. Because of this, the position they take toward individual team members, from that team member's perspective, feels something like this:

"Great job, great job, great job, okay now you're fired."

As a manager, we want to be careful that we are safely giving individual team members critical feedback in such a way they can accept that feedback, metabolize what they've learned, and evolve as value-driven professionals.

The key to giving good feedback is to always, always be *for* the team member you are instructing. A team member that senses blank judgment is not going to be receptive to feedback.

We've all seen basketball and football coaches get angry at their players and directly criticize them, sometimes on national television. And yet, most players still adore the coach who so passionately corrected their behavior. Why? It's because of what we didn't see, the fact that that coach has made it extremely clear they are *for* the player and they want the player to win in sports and in life.

Any person will willingly take (and hunger for) criticism from a manager who is undoubtedly for them.

When giving critical feedback, here are some general rules to follow:

1. Give the feedback soon.
2. Ask the team member to explore what happened with you.
3. "Rewrite" the scenario in the team member's mind using a different approach (and explore better approaches with them) so the team member knows how to do it right the next time.
4. Remind the team member that you are for them and want them and the team to succeed.

It is not enough to let a team member know they have failed. A team member needs to know they have failed and then be given specific instructions allowing them to succeed in the future.

As managers, if we just want to use people, we will praise them for their successes and then get rid of them if they fail too often. But if we are for people, we praise them for their successes and teach them practical tools that will help them succeed over and over. How? By offering praise and constructive feedback.

> **Here's Today's Business Made Simple Tip of the Day**
>
> Offer praise and constructive feedback to each member of your team.

DAY FIFTY-FIVE
How to Manage People—Be More Than a Cheer-leader, Be a Coach

A good manager is a coach, not just a cheerleader.

A coach and a cheerleader have one thing in common. They both want the team to win.

And that is all they have in common.

Sadly, when most business leaders hire a business coach, they don't get a coach, they get a cheerleader.

Coaches transfer their business knowledge to their team members and thus duplicate themselves within a growing organization. Even if team members don't want to become managers, their understanding of how and why the manager is doing things the way they are doing things creates a sense of understanding and ownership. Cheerleaders cheer teams on while coaches instruct the team about processes that lead to victory.

There is nothing wrong with a cheerleader, of course, but a cheerleader is not enough to lead a team (or an individual) to success.

The difference between a coach and a cheerleader is that while a cheerleader cheers you on, a coach gives you specific instructions and objectives that help you succeed, then helps you learn and employ those frameworks on the job.

Professionals who are lucky enough to have a good business coach are destined for success.

Let's make sure our team members have a coach. A good manager knows how to coach a team.

Here are the five characteristics of a good business coach:

1. They want each member of the team to succeed in their job and in their career.

2. They have an honest, objective assessment of each team member's skills and motivation.

3. They teach practical frameworks and skills to their team members rather than expecting them to know things they've never been taught.

4. They offer routine, safe, and constructive feedback so team members can get better.

5. They praise a team member's individual success and affirm the transformation of their identity.

Imagine working hard to make the high school basketball team. On the first day of practice, the coach lines the team up and explains that the key to a winning season is simple—that you as a team must score more points than the other team. The coach then explains that if you don't score more points than the other team, you will be held accountable. But don't worry, because if you do, you will be praised and rewarded.

And that's it.

This team is obviously destined for ruin. Why? Because the team does not have a coach, the team has a cheerleader.

A coach explains to the team how the game works, assesses each team member's specific talents and puts them in the right position, develops each team member by teaching them practical, repeatable behaviors that will improve their game, and then guides them each into personal transformation so they can become the best basketball players they can be.

In the world of business, few professionals even know effective business frameworks in the first place, much less teach them to their team members. Most businesses don't have managers (much less coaches); they have cheerleaders. This has to change.

As a manager, teach the frameworks you've learned in this book to your team members. Help them understand how the machine of a business works and let them know what valuable skill sets they already have and what skill sets they need to improve upon.

While team members like cheerleaders, they like *and respect* coaches. A good manager is a good coach.

Here's Today's Business Made Simple Tip of the Day

Coach each member of your team by teaching them frameworks they can use to succeed.

A Value-Driven Professional

* *Increase your personal economic value by mastering each core competency.*

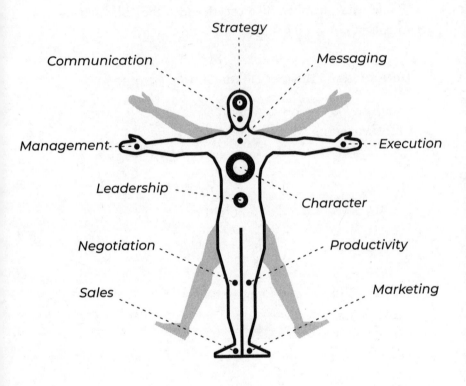

CHAPTER ELEVEN

EXECUTION MADE SIMPLE

INTRODUCTION

Since we've learned the character of a competent professional, created our mission statement and guiding principles, increased our personal productivity, realized how a business really works, clarified our message, learned to give a good presentation, understood how a marketing sales funnel works, learned a framework to help us sell, how to be a better negotiator, and a framework that allows us to be a much-respected manager, let's learn to run an execution system that ensures our teams are passionate and productive.

There is not a single characteristic I value more in a team member than their ability to execute.

We can sit and talk about ideas all day, but it's only the ideas that turn into products that are sold to customers that move a company forward.

Now that we know how to manage people by creating good processes, how do we make sure we execute on those processes?

Without an execution system, team members work in a fog.

A value-driven professional who can instill and manage an execution system lifts the fog and brings the light.

The highest-paid team member on my staff manages the execution system. Why? Because they ensure every member of my team is operating at the highest level.

A company does not make money until the product is sitting on the shelf, the salesforce is equipped with the resources they need, and the marketing campaign is being executed. Every ounce of energy a group of people spends is wasted unless the job is actually done and the product is returning revenue and profit. An enormous amount of energy is wasted every year for lack of a good execution system.

If Management Made Simple is the design of a process that creates the profitable output of products and services, Execution Made Simple is how you manage the repeatable (and relational) exchanges involved in those processes.

The steps to the Execution Made Simple framework are:

1. Hold a launch meeting to launch a project or initiative.
2. Have each team member fill out a "one-pager."
3. Hold weekly "speed checks."
4. Keep score and measure your success.
5. Celebrate your team's victories.

A master of business knows how to drive a process through to completion. Running the Execution Made Simple process will transform you into the team member every organization needs—a team member who can get things done.

DAY FIFTY-SIX
How to Execute—Hold a Launch Meeting

Hold a launch meeting to launch the project or initiative.

You've been entrusted with a project. Finally. You've been waiting years to be given this level of responsibility, and you know if you get the job done, you'll stand out in the organization. This could mean a raise, a promotion, or even being made the head of a department. So what do you do next?

If you're like most people, you'll make a giant, all-encompassing to-do list, and while you might ask others for help on a few of the critical objectives, you'll carry most of the weight yourself to make sure everything is done right.

As the weeks and months go by, you become fuzzy about what the boss actually wanted and then you're hit with a minor crisis in your department. Managing the crisis takes priority over the new project you were asked to launch and so you put it on the back burner for a moment until you can come back to it.

After a year, the project, once so important, comes up in a meeting and you sheepishly explain other priorities seemed to have crept in.

The boss is disappointed and mentally labels you as middle management at best.

Sadly, the boss is right. At the highest level of any organization sit people who may or may not be creative, smart, passionate, or even hardworking. But every single one of them knows how to get things done.

So how do we get things done?

The way to get things done is to break the project down into its parts and then manage the completion of those parts using an execution system.

When an important project comes down the line, do not trust your gut or your instincts as to how to accomplish the tasks. Instead, follow a careful checklist along with a few routine processes to ensure the project gets done and gets done on time.

The first thing you want to do at your launch meeting is to fill out a "project scope" worksheet. You can find this free worksheet at ExecutionMadeSimple.com. The four questions on the project scope worksheet will guide you to:

1. **Set a clear view of success.** In crystal clear language, define exactly what needs to get done. Make sure the success is measurable, so you know exactly when it is accomplished.

2. **Assign the leaders.** Make sure every aspect of the project has a clearly assigned leader. Somebody should be directly responsible if a component of the project is not accomplished.

3. **Identify resources needed.** List all the resources you and your team will need to accomplish this project. Assign people to collect those resources.

4. **Create a timeline with key milestones.** In a public place, display a timeline of when major milestones will be accomplished.

If you are including a team in your execution strategy session, answer all four questions and create any necessary collateral in a single meeting.

At the end of the meeting, make sure to announce that the launch of this project is official. It will serve your team to have a psychological memory of a moment in which the project became real. This is not an idea, a thought, a wish, or a dream. This is a project that has been launched with the expectation that it will be driven through to completion.

The key here is to keep the fog of fuzzy priorities at bay. Every person should know what part of the project they are directly responsible for, when it needs to be done, and why it matters.

Clarity is a prerequisite for commitment. Unless you are clear about what needs to be done, by whom, and by when, the project will fail.

> ### Here's Today's Business Made Simple Tip of the Day
>
> When holding a launch meeting, fill out a project scope worksheet that will help you set a clear view of success, assign the leaders, identify resources needed, and create a timeline with key milestones.

DAY FIFTY-SEVEN
How to Execute—Instill the One-Pager

Have each member of the team fill out a one-pager.

After launching the project, every member of your team should be crystal clear about two things: the priorities for their department and their personal priorities.

No matter how successful your initial meeting went, the fog of fuzzy priorities will come for you and your team, and its one goal is to keep you from getting the job done.

The second step in the Execution Made Simple framework, then, is to assign a one-pager to each member of your team (see Figure 11.1). Again, you can download a free one-pager template at ExecutionMadeSimple.com.

It's a good idea to have each team member fill out the one-pager during the launch meeting. Don't worry about getting it right the first time. The one-pager is an evolving document.

NAME

MY DEPARTMENT'S TOP 5 PRIORITIES

1. _____
2. _____
3. _____
4. _____
5. _____

MY PERSONAL PRIORITIES

1. _____
2. _____
3. _____
4. _____
5. _____

MY DEVELOPMENT PLAN

1. _____
2. _____
3. _____

FIGURE 11.1

As the project evolves and more and more tasks are completed, priorities will shift and change.

At my company, we've printed and laminated large one-pagers so they hang near every desk. Why? Because nearly every hour of every day, people forget what their priorities are.

In the whirlwind of ringing phones and approaching deadlines, the brain has a difficult time remembering what matters.

Each one-pager is intentionally simple. You and your team members will simply review the "clear view of success" determined during the launch meeting, then list the top five priorities for each department and the top five personal priorities for each individual.

Hanging each team member's one-pager in a public place allows teams to constantly analyze each other's priorities to invite feedback and keep everybody accountable to actually accomplish them.

You can use digital one-pagers if you like, but at my company we prefer paper. I like for a one-pager to be visible at all times so we always know what to focus on at a glance, no matter what's happening on our phone or computer.

If you like, laminate the one-pagers and hang them near each desk so each team member's is visible.

Once the one-pagers are complete, everybody will know and be accountable to accomplish very specific tasks.

> **Here's Today's Business Made Simple Tip of the Day**
>
> Have each team member fill out a one-pager that establishes their personal and department priorities.

DAY FIFTY-EIGHT
How to Execute—Hold Weekly Speed Checks

Hold weekly speed checks.

Many projects die directly after they are launched. This happens for two reasons:

1. People get distracted with other important tasks and obligations.
2. People forget the details and importance of the new project.

In order to achieve the "clear view of success" that was determined at the launch of the project, routines and habits will have to be created, all designed to finish the job.

Habits are only developed when actions are performed repeatedly.

To turn actions into habits, every pertinent member of a team should review their actions and priorities in a weekly meeting called a speed check. The meeting is called a speed check because it's designed to keep momentum going by being fast and focused.

Think of a speed check as not unlike a huddle in a football game. This is not a strategy session. This is a quick meeting to make sure everybody on the team knows the play and their specific role in the play.

Hold the speed check at a fixed time each week and don't skip it. It's better to hold the meeting standing so it doesn't go long.

Make sure every team member has their laminated one-pager with them during the meeting so they can make adjustments as needed.

Make sure every team member has prepared written answers to routine questions that are asked each week.

Having your team members come prepared with written statements ensures the meeting remains brief and that necessary actions are further memorialized.

The structure of a speed check should cover three review statements and three questions:

Three Review Statements

1. Read the "clear view of success" statement for the given project.
2. Review the priorities of the team member's department.
3. Review the team member's personal priorities.

Three Questions

1. Answer the question "What has each team member gotten done?"
2. Answer the question "What is each team member going to do next?"
3. Answer the question "What's blocking any team members from making progress?"

That third question is an invitation for any team member to ask for help. One of the jobs of a leader is to remove blockers that are stopping team members from making progress.

A team member should walk away from a meeting feeling inspired and directed. A manager should walk away from a speed check with a short list of things to do that remove the blockers from individual team members.

The speed check should not go more than twenty minutes, which is why it's best done while standing. Sitting down and catching up will drag this meeting on and likely lead to less, not more, progress toward the clear view of success.

It is critical not to miss or skip meetings. Skipping meetings will almost ensure the clear view of success is not accomplished.

If you are not able to attend a speed check in person, perform the speed check over the phone or remotely via virtual conference software.

If a project is critical or during a crisis, consider holding speed checks every day rather than once each week. Even if priorities and tasks seem to "always be the same" because you are meeting so often, it doesn't matter. The activity-to-output ratio will still increase dramatically because you are keeping the fog of fuzzy priorities away.

If you fail to hold speed check meetings, your execution plan will not work and your project or initiative will likely die.

Momentum must be maintained, and routine speed checks are how you maintain that momentum.

Here's Today's Business Made Simple Tip of the Day

Hold weekly speed checks with every member of your team to maintain momentum and accountability.

DAY FIFTY-NINE
How to Execute—Keep Score

Keep score and measure your success.

People need to measure their progress in order to be healthy and happy. Expecting people to excel without giving them a way to measure their progress will drive them crazy and negatively affect morale.

There is nothing you can do to boost morale and energize a team more than to have everybody on that team understand the rules of the game, feel that they are being coached to victory, and have proof of their progress on a public scoreboard.

The fourth aspect of the Execution Made Simple framework, then, is to create a public scoreboard.

How many sales calls was each person on the sales team expected to make this week and how did they do? How many hours were the members of the content team supposed to spend writing new content? How many customer service tickets were the customer service representatives able to answer?

To create a scoreboard, sit down with each team member and analyze the priorities of their department. Break down those priorities into repeatable tasks that, if accomplished, will ensure those priorities are met. Then measure those repeatable tasks on a scoreboard.

If your developers check sections of code off a list of needs, how many sections of code could the coder you're talking to normally check off in a week?

Work with your team members to create the department's scoreboard.

Questions like *how would you like to be measured in your progress toward our objectives?* are important so that each division has a sense of ownership over the overall project. Team members should be comfortable and even excited about how they are going to be measured.

You will be tempted to measure lag measures, but don't. Again, lag measures are measures like total sales, new leads, products shipped, and so on. Once total sales are in, there's nothing you can do to increase those sales. It's too late.

Instead, measure lead measures. Again, lead measures are actions your team members can take to affect lag measures. If your lag measure is total sales, a lead measure might be sales calls that cause total sales to happen. So measure sales calls on your scoreboard rather than sales.

It's okay to measure more than one lead measure on your team member's speed check sheet, but be careful not to measure more than three items. If you measure more than three items, people have difficulty knowing which of their repeatable tasks are really important. The most important tasks directly affect the overall objectives of the division they work within.

Make sure to include a short review of the scoreboard in your weekly speed check (see Figure 11.2). This should take no more than a few seconds. After assessing the score, ask if there's anything the division can do differently to improve the score.

If you don't let people know how they are doing, morale will suffer. Nobody likes to run in a dense fog. They want to

SCOREBOARD

| Sales calls | 400 |
| Lunch meetings | 6 |

FIGURE 11.2

know where and how fast they are going based on visible points of demarcation.

Again, when you give your people scoreboards to measure their progress, you're doing more than increasing their productivity; you're increasing their overall well-being.

Here's Today's Business Made Simple Tip of the Day

Create a customized scoreboard for each division so every team member knows how their division is doing.

DAY SIXTY
How to Execute—Celebrate Your Team's Victories

Celebrate your team's victories.

To lead an execution system, it's important that we celebrate our team's victories and affirm their transformation into value-driven professionals.

Creating a routine of celebrating wins is paramount to a team's success.

Sadly, many competitive leaders don't notice wins.

It makes sense. Because we are so hooked on winning, when we finally accomplish our goal we waste no time celebrating and simply move on to the next challenge.

But most people are not so self-motivated. They need to be acknowledged. And they need to hear from somebody in authority that the win was truly a win.

There's a scene at the end of most movies called "the affirmation of transformation." This scene involves two principal characters, the guide and the hero. After the hero has overcome the challenge to accomplish the objective, the guide steps in, looks the hero in the eye, and says, "You've changed. You're different now. You're stronger, more competent, more capable. Congratulations. You did it."

Yoda and Obi-Wan come back to nod their approval at Luke. Lionel, the drama teacher in *The King's Speech*, says to King George that he is a great king. Mr. Miagi affirms to Daniel that he is indeed a champion in *The Karate Kid*.

Celebrating an individual's win is how you let them know they've changed, that they've become more competent and capable. Celebrating wins is a critical and necessary routine if we want to develop our people.

In order to celebrate wins, you'll need to:

1. Notice them.
2. Memorialize them.
3. Acknowledge those responsible.

We must start noticing wins. In order to do this, we use our scoreboards. When we surpass a measure on our scoreboard, we celebrate.

Second, we have to memorialize these wins. The celebration should be relative to the success, of course. If a team member hits their weekly goal, an excited high five is important. And if a significant, monthly, overall company goal is hit, an office lunch, cake, happy hour, or something of the sort may be in order.

As the leader, though, make sure to memorialize the celebration in words. Our team members cannot read our minds. Standing up during the lunch and letting everybody know what we are celebrating is important or the celebration won't actually boost morale and contribute to the team members transforming the way they think of themselves.

Third, you'll want to specifically acknowledge those who are directly responsible for the win. This is your chance to look the heroes in the eye and affirm their transformation. They are stronger than they used to be, more competent, and more capable. Let them know they have changed and become even more valuable to the team.

Be careful not to celebrate non-wins. It may be tempting to celebrate getting close to a difficult goal, but doing so will dilute the power of a real celebration. Being disappointed because we did not hit a goal is an important part of life. People pleasers will want to rush in and offer support and celebration for near-victories, but such support isn't helpful to a team's development.

Feeling the difference between a win and a loss makes a win feel that much better. Save up the celebrations for actual victories. After all, spiking the ball at the five yard line is called a fumble.

If you celebrate wins and learn from disappointing performances, the team will constantly evolve and get better. We all love playing games and we all love to win at the games we play. Keeping a scoreboard and celebrating victories makes work fun, productive, and transformative.

> ### Here's Today's Business Made Simple Tip of the Day
>
> Celebrate wins by noticing them, memorializing them, and acknowledging those responsible and you will increase morale and drive performance.

CONGRATULATIONS

When you bought (or were given) this book, you likely thought it was going to be a simple daily reflection, but it was much more than that. This was a business education like few people ever receive. If you finished the book, you learned the very basics that it takes to become a value-driven professional and you also learned sixty business strategies they hardly teach in college. If you want to become an even better value-driven professional, start the process over and do it all again (or hire one of our certified coaches). The more you affirm what you've learned, the more economic value you will have on the open market, I promise.

The fact that so many people pay $50,000 per year to attend college, leave college with an enormous amount of debt, are unable to buy their first home until they are in their thirties (which costs them a decade of equity and accumulating wealth), then start to be burdened with medical bills and more debt only a few decades later is sad. Our students deserve better. An education shouldn't cost them their economic success or freedom. I believe if you master what is in this book, you are of extreme value. You should not have to take on debt to become what the market needs you to be.

Congratulations on becoming a value-driven professional. You are what the market has been awaiting for a long time. Now let's put this knowledge to work solving the world's problems.

To take a deep dive into Business Made Simple courses,
get access to Business Made Simple online courses at
BusinessMadeSimple.com.

To find a certified coach who can coach you to
start or scale your business, visit
HireACoach.com.

To become a Business Made Simple certified coach,
visit CertifiedBusinessCoach.com.

To verify that your coach or facilitator is certified by
Business Made Simple, check for their name at
HireACoach.com.

USE THIS BOOK TO DRIVE A CULTURE
OF LEARNING AND DEVELOPMENT.

Get a copy of this book for each member of your team, ask your team members to register at BusinessMadeSimple.com/daily, and enjoy the results that come from a team of value-driven professionals.

USE THIS BOOK AS AN ON-RAMPING
TOOL FOR YOUR ORGANIZATION.

Instruct all new hires to go through the Business Made Simple sixty-day process as part of your on-ramping protocol.

Did you buy more than one thousand copies of this book in order to develop your team?

Each year, heads of many large organizations meet at Donald Miller's home to discuss their challenges and share their successes.

Visit www.LeadershipAdvantage.com to learn more.

ACKNOWLEDGMENTS

Without the brilliant team at Business Made Simple, this book would not have been possible. My team wakes up every morning knowing that the training we create helps tens of thousands of businesses get more done, grow their revenue, and provide better jobs for more people. And at a fraction of the price as college. Thanks for being motivated to disrupt America's university system, as well as corporate learning and development. And for believing that everybody deserves a life-changing business education.

Specifically, thanks to Koula Calahan, Dr. JJ Peterson, and Doug Keim, my content team colleagues who added much to this book.

I have always enjoyed my relationship with the publishers and editors at HarperCollins Leadership. Special thanks to Sara Kendrick, who carefully edited this book along with Jeff Farr, and the team who worked to edit, typeset, and package this story into a book. I'd like to thank Sicily Axton and the HCL marketing team for their support.

Finally, thank you for caring enough about your own development or the development of your entire team to buy this book. We believe the simple knowledge it takes to grow a business should not exist behind a paywall that demands tens of thousands of dollars. The tens of thousands of successful businesses that exist around the world are the greatest tool we have to combat poverty. Without you, the world would suffer. Here's to the success of your business.

INDEX

ABOUT THE AUTHOR

Donald Miller has helped more than fifty thousand businesses clarify their marketing messages so their companies grow. He's the CEO of Business Made Simple, the host of the *Business Made Simple* podcast, and the author of several books, including the bestsellers *Building a StoryBrand* and *Marketing Made Simple*.

@DonaldMiller on Instagram and Twitter